ESTATE DOCUMENTS
AT
LAMBETH PALACE LIBRARY

ESTATE DOCUMENTS
AT
LAMBETH PALACE
LIBRARY

a short catalogue by

JANE SAYERS

LEICESTER UNIVERSITY PRESS
1965

*Printed at The Broadwater Press Ltd
Welwyn Garden City, Herts., for
Leicester University Press*

ARRANGEMENT AND CONTENTS

INTRODUCTION

THE large collection of Estate Documents at Lambeth may be divided into two sections. The first section, which is described below, consists of court rolls and books, account rolls, terriers, rentals, valors, and extents or surveys. All rolls are included here: it is for the most part a collection of medieval records. The other section, hereafter referred to as Archiepiscopal Temporalities to save confusion, is composed mainly of documents which were at the Church Commissioners until April to December 1960, being held by the Vicar General's Office on behalf of the Receiver General. It consists of volumes and loose documents and contains conveyances, leases, surveys, title deeds, rentals, accounts, vouchers, and estate *memoranda* and correspondence. There are no rolls or court documents in the Archiepiscopal Temporalities section, and nothing dating from before 1535.

The Estate Document Collection [section one] now numbers 2,073 rolls, books and items.[1] When in 1877 A. J. Horwood inspected on behalf of the Historical Manuscripts Commission "about fifty bags containing . . . several hundred parchment and paper rolls", he identified most of them as manorial documents which he felt should be arranged and catalogued.[2] He does not refer to, and evidently did not know of, a manuscript catalogue of the rolls, made in 1762 by A. C. Ducarel. This "Catalogue of the Old Court Rolls, Computus Ballivorum & other ancient Deeds, Chartae etc. etc. preserved in the manuscript Library at Lambeth" is now Additional MS. 5707 in the British Museum, to whom it was bequeathed by Sir William Burrell, the antiquary. It is not known how Burrell, who died in 1796, came by it.[3] The catalogue is the first extant list of the records of the temporalities of the see of Canterbury: it was arranged on a strictly chronological basis,[4] and it is recorded in 1762 that Archbishop Secker paid Dr Ducarel £16 2s. for compiling it.[5] In 1880 a new catalogue was made for Archbishop Tait by the firm of record agents known as S. A. Moore and R. E. G. Kirk, who listed 1773 documents.[6] A summary of the court rolls only, in this very useful list, was printed by N. J. Hone, in *The Manor and Manorial Records* [The Antiquary's Books, London, 1906], 285–97. The rolls which Moore and Kirk numbered and catalogued were principally such records as had been left behind in Morton's

---

[1] For a list of the numbers and their significance, see Appendix A. There are also some manuscripts belonging to this collection, see Appendix B, 80.

[2] *H.M.C. 6th Report*, London, 1877, 522.

[3] For Burrell, see *D.N.B.* VII, London, 1886, 442.

[4] "The rolls had at one time been sorted into chronological order, but very roughly, and with many errors and exceptions to the rule" [S. A. Moore and R. E. G. Kirk, MS. Calendar of Court Rolls, Ministers' Accounts, Rentals & other Rolls and Documents preserved in the Archiepiscopal Library at Lambeth Palace, 1880, Introduction].

[5] Lambeth Palace Library MS. 1483, f. 103, 1 June 1762.

[6] See above note 4, and Appendix A.

Tower when the Ecclesiastical Commissioners took over the administration of the archiepiscopal estates and their records, but they also included a number of strays from the classes of document which make up the *Cartae Miscellaneae*, and a group of Commonwealth presentation deeds closely related to others bound up as MSS. 944–7, and still others which were later found loose in Morton's Tower. These have now been restored to their appropriate classes.

Of the documents taken by the Ecclesiastical Commissioners in the late nineteenth century, those relating to Lambeth, Croydon and Waddon, and Dover Priory [nos. 1902–37, 1945–72, 1980–98, 2000–5] were retained at their Millbank repository.[7] The others, relating to archiepiscopal properties mainly grouped, and mainly in Kent [nos. 1774–1881 and 1884–93], were deposited by the Commissioners in 1889 at the Public Record Office, where they were numbered and listed.[8] Both these two collections were brought back to Lambeth in July 1959 and January 1960. The documents listed below consist of all the estate documents in Moore and Kirk's list [nos. 1–451 and 453–1429 together with certain numbers out of their section entitled Miscellaneous Rolls],[9] the two Church Commissioners' groups, and further rolls and documents which have since come to light. Nothing of the section of Archiepiscopal Temporalities, which was deposited by the Commissioners between April and May and in December 1960, has been included. Furthermore, nothing has been taken out of that section and put into this, but a few strays have been replaced there.

Professor Du Boulay has described the radical change which took place in the composition of the Canterbury estates between the Valor of 1535 and the accession of Elizabeth in 1558.[10] In the main the enquirer into Canterbury lands before "the great exchange" will find all he needs in the following catalogue, but anyone interested in the manors acquired as a result of these exchanges will need to consult both collections. Leases, surrenders etc., for manors which have remained in archiepiscopal hands throughout the changes of the sixteenth century, such as Lambeth, will be found in the Archiepiscopal Temporalities section. Similarly, surviving medieval title deeds to archiepiscopal properties are not included here, but are in the *Cartae Miscellaneae* series and in the cartularies of the see of Canterbury, such as MS. 1212.[11]

For the present list, the descriptions given in previous lists where they exist, have been checked, stereotyped, corrected where necessary, and in some cases amplified. Many fragments have been placed, and several accounts etc., which had been swallowed up into the *Cartae Miscellaneae* collection, have now been restored to their counterparts.[12] Each document has been classified under the owner of the manor at the time when the record was made. Further details are then given and the names of subsidiary places. An index has been provided. The documents

[7] See Appendix B, 78–9.   [8] See Appendix B, 76–8.
[9] The number 452 was not used in their list.
[10] F. R. H. Du Boulay, "Archbishop Cranmer and the Canterbury Temporalities", *E.H.R.* lxvii [1952], 19–36.
[11] For other cartularies of the see of Canterbury, see G. R. C. Davis, *Medieval Cartularies of Great Britain*, London, 1958, 20.
[12] See Appendix B, Group III, 79.

fall naturally into several sections and the present list is arranged on the basis of these sections. The scheme was devised by Mrs D. M. Owen, to whom the present catalogue owes much. Mrs Owen left Lambeth before the scheme was completed and she must not therefore be held responsible for the details of its present form.

The largest group consists of Archiepiscopal Records. These are:

A. COURT ROLLS (1) Individual properties by counties: Hertfordshire, Kent, Middlesex, Surrey and Sussex.

                (2) Grouped properties for Kent.

B. ACCOUNT ROLLS (1) Individual properties by counties: Bucks., Essex, Herts., Kent, Surrey and Sussex.

                (2) Household Account.

                (3) Valor.

                (4) Rental and Survey.

                (5) Ministers' Accounts: various manors.

                (6) Ministers' Accounts by bailiwicks.

                (7) Receivers' Accounts by bailiwicks.

                (8) Ministers' Accounts: general.

                (9) Receivers' Accounts: general.

             (10) Liberty of the Archbishop.

They are of immense use and interest particularly for the history of the counties of Kent, Sussex and Surrey. Roll no. 2068 is of immediate note. It was acquired for the Library in June 1963, and it seems fitting to record here the generosity of The Most Reverend Dr Michael Ramsey, Lord Archbishop of Canterbury, A. R. Neelands, Esq., The Church Commissioners, The Friends of the National Libraries, Callard and Bowser Limited, Kodak Limited, The Nestlé Company Limited, J. Sainsbury Limited, *et alii*, who made this purchase possible. The document is a late thirteenth-century survey and rental of the possessions of the archbishopric, based probably on an earlier and fuller one, which was made at the beginning of the thirteenth century, and which no longer survives, save in a fifteenth-century copy among the archives of the Dean and Chapter of Canterbury [MS. E 24]. It was at Lambeth in 1634 when it occupied a place on shelf no. 31 in "the paper study" being described as a "Roll of Survey in 4° Johannis".[13] With the execution of Archbishop Laud in 1645 it disappeared from the Lambeth archives together with other valuable documents. It has now been restored to its rightful home amongst the Archbishop's muniments.

Another section contains a certain number of Christ Church, Canterbury, records, both of the Prior and convent and of the Dean and Chapter. They consist principally of account rolls of certain obedientiaries, notably the almoner

[13] D. M. Barratt, "The Library of John Selden and its later history", *Bodleian Library Record* III, no. 31 [March 1951], 138, citing MS. Tanner 88 f. 24.

and cellarer, with court and account rolls of manors in Devon and Kent belonging to these obedientiaries and the sacrist, and some grouped court rolls of the Dean and Chapter. Besides this there is a small group of rolls for the Prior and convent of Rochester and for the Kentish religious houses of Faversham, St Sexburga's Minster, St Augustine's Canterbury, and St Radegund's Dover, which were temporarily or permanently in archiepiscopal hands after the Dissolution.

There is finally a large group of accounts and court rolls of manors belonging to the Bishop of Bath and Wells and the Dean and Chapter of Wells, the Bishop of Chichester, the Bishop of Ely and the Prior and convent of Ely, the Bishop of Winchester and the Prior and convent of Winchester, the Bishop of Worcester and the Prior and convent of Worcester, and the Prior and convent of St Benet of Hulme, Norfolk.[14] All of these rolls were in the Library when Dr Ducarel made his list in 1762. The Bath and Wells documents may have come from Laud's brief tenure of that see [1626–8]. They include a household roll of Bishop Ralph of Shrewsbury, diocesan of Bath and Wells, dating from 1337–8, which has been edited by J. Armitage Robinson and A. Hamilton Thompson in *Collectanea* [Somerset Record Society xxxix, 1924]. The Dean and Chapter of Wells' rolls presumably came through the same source. The Chichester documents, all of which belong to the years 1429–30, appear to be some of the records of a long vacancy in that bishopric, 1429–31, after John Rickingale's death and the quashing of the election of Thomas Brouns[15] during which the rights of the Archbishop of Canterbury "sede vacante" were enforced. The Ely and Worcester rolls appear to have come to Lambeth after Bourgchier [1435–43] and Whitgift [1577–83] held these sees before translation to Canterbury. The confused history of the see of Winchester after Gardiner's deprivation and trial at Lambeth in 1550–1 perhaps explains the presence of some Winchester records. Those of Norwich, which are chiefly and possibly entirely of manors once belonging to St Benet of Hulme, which with its possessions was granted by Henry VIII to the Bishop of Norwich in 1536,[16] must have come in with several papal bulls in MSS. Tenison 643 and 644 and with the charters of that house which are included in *Cartae Miscellaneae* and which seem to have appeared in the period of Edmund Gibson's librarianship [c. 1700–7], possibly through his friendship with Thomas Tanner, successively Chancellor of Norwich diocese, commissary of the archdeaconries of Norfolk and Sudbury, and later Archdeacon of Norfolk.[17]

Further rolls of archiepiscopal properties are among the records of the Court

[14] A letter survives at Lambeth from Sir Henry Maxwell Lyte to Canon Claude Jenkins, dated 4 March 1911, in which Maxwell Lyte said that he had "sometimes wondered" how these various groups got to Lambeth.

[15] *Handbook of British Chronology*, 217.

[16] "In all the preceding classes there are many rolls relative to the Abbey of St Benet of Hulme and its possessions in Norfolk. Many of these gave us a great deal of trouble before we could identify them, and their existence can hardly have been suspected until now. How they came into this collection has not been discovered" [Moore & Kirk, MS. Calendar, Introduction].

[17] Further documents from St Benet of Hulme, including a number of rolls, are in the Bodleian Library, see *Calendar of Charters & Rolls preserved in the Bodleian Library*, ed. W. H. Turner, Oxford, 1878, 239–49; the donor of these was Thomas Tanner.

of Augmentations at the Public Record Office, and are to be found listed in *Lists & Indexes: V Ministers' Accounts* I, 422–5, *XXXIV Ministers' Accounts* II, 63, and *VI Court Rolls* I, 222–3, 300–2, and 307. Others are at Maidstone. They include some ministers' accounts for 1488–9, and for 1496–7,[18] and a grouped roll of the Archbishop's manors, 1638–9,[19] together with separate rolls for some of his manors, such as Aldington and Wrotham, and for the hundreds of Calehill, Gillingham and Teynham.[20] The main series of the manorial court and account rolls of the Prior and convent of Christ Church, Canterbury, and the Dean and Chapter of the Cathedral Church, are amongst the muniments of the Dean and Chapter at Canterbury.

Both the court rolls and the account rolls of the Archbishop illustrate historically the growth of an administrative system, which was gradually made more perfect. The separate court rolls gave way by 1511 to grouped ones for all the properties, although the keeping of separate rolls or books was not entirely superseded. The account rolls, perhaps, reflect even more strikingly a process of gradual refinement and development. The earliest surviving account rolls for the archbishopric are in the form of general statements for all the properties, as no. 1193 dating from 1236-7. The old pipe roll form disappeared during the 1270s and was replaced by a great series of individual accounts for the separate manors. In Archbishop Pecham's time the manors were grouped in six bailiwicks and so began the series of ministers' rolls. Next a receiver was placed over one or more bailiwicks, and his accounts brought together the cash receipts from the local ministers. A further step was the appointment of a Steward of the Archbishop's Liberty.[21] At the beginning of Elizabeth's reign the division into bailiwicks was abolished. The whole of the ministers' accounts of the see were enrolled on one roll in each year, and at the same time a Receiver General was appointed whose yearly accounts comprised the whole see. The Receiver General administered the estates on behalf of the Archbishop of Canterbury, who remained a great temporal lord until the properties of the see were vested in the Ecclesiastical Commissioners on 6 September 1862, the day of the death of Archbishop Sumner.

Michaelmas Day 1963   JANE SAYERS

[18] See Felix Hull, *Guide to the Kent County Archives Office*, Maidstone, 1958, Part IV, Estate and Family Archives, 182 and 139.
[19] *Guide to the Kent County Archives Office*, 187.
[20] *Ibid.*, Part IV, more especially 139–223.
[21] On the development of the medieval financial system, see F. R. H. Du Boulay, "The Archbishop as Territorial Magnate", in *Medieval Records of the Archbishop of Canterbury*, London, 1962, 63–4.

ABBREVIATIONS

al.	= alias
att[s].	= attachment[s]
c.	= circa
CC	= Church Commissioners
CM	= Cartae Miscellaneae
Cant.Cath.MS.	= Canterbury Cathedral Manuscript
cent.	= century
conc.	= concerning
D.N.B.	= Dictionary of National Biography
E.H.R.	= English Historical Review
Epiph.	= Epiphany
f[f].	= folio[s]
fol.	= following
H.M.C.	= Historical Manuscripts Commission
incl.	= including
K. & H.	= David Knowles & R. Neville Hadcock, *Medieval Religious Houses—England & Wales*, London, 1953
m[m].	= membrane[s]
Mich.	= Michaelmas
misc.	= miscellaneous
Mon.	= Sir William Dugdale, *Monasticon Anglicanum* ed. Caley, Ellis & Bandinel, 6 vols. in 8 pts., London, 1846
p[p].	= page[s]
Place Names Sussex	= A. Mawer & F. M. Stenton, *The Place-Names of Sussex* 2 pts., English Place Name Society vi & vii, Cambridge, 1929–30
P.R.O.	= Public Record Office
temp.	= tempore
unid.	= unidentified
W.A.M.	= Westminster Abbey Muniments

NOTES

(1) For Kentish place names,

J. K. Wallenberg, *The Place-Names of Kent*, Uppsala, 1934,

Edward Hasted, *The History and Topographical Survey of the County of Kent*
2nd ed. 12 vols., Canterbury, 1797–1801,

and the 2½-inch *Ordnance Survey Maps* for the county, have been used.

(2) Square brackets round the date, e.g. [1467–8], and round the main entry,
e.g. [Reeve], denote uncertainty.

(3) Dates are given in the modern form.

I

ARCHIEPISCOPAL ESTATES

A. COURT ROLLS

(1) *Individual properties by counties:*
Herts., Kent, Middlesex, Surrey and Sussex

Herts.

Name of place				Document numbers		
TRING				nos. 1075–6		
1075	Courts			1414–15	5 mm.	
1076	Court and view			1415 Easter	2 mm.	

Kent

ALDINGTON				nos. 136–8		
136	Courts [Views at Bircholt, Langport in Lydd, Palstre in Wittersham, St Martin's and Worth]			1449–50	4 mm.	
137	Courts [Courts and views at Kinghamford (Bishopsbourne), Loningborough (Lyminge), Petham, and Heane (Saltwood). Views at Bircholt, Lydd, Oxney, Palstre, St Martin's, and Sibersnoth in Orlestone]			1488–9	7 mm.	
138	Same, omitting Kinghamford [Bishopsbourne]			1536–7	4 mm.	
BEXLEY				no. 233		
233	Courts and views [Courts at Northfleet, hundreds at Toltintrough, views at Cliffe, Earde in Crayford, Foots Cray, Halfley and West Preston]			1495–6	7 mm.	
BISHOPSBOURNE				no. 283		
283	Courts and views			1448–9	1 m.	
BOUGHTON UNDER BLEAN				nos. 272–81, 1796–8, 1801, 1804, 1806, 1808, 1829, 2019		
272	Courts, hundreds and views			1448–9	3 mm.	
273	,,	,,	,,	,,	1449–50	3 mm.
274	,,	,,	,,	,,	1469–70	2 mm.
275	,,	,,	,,	,,	1472–3	2 mm.
276	,,	,,	,,	,,	1489–90	2 mm.
277	,,	,,	,,	,,	1501–2	2 mm.
278	,,	,,	,,	,,	1506–7	2 mm.
279	,,	,,	,,	,,	1510–11	11 pp. 4 atts.

280	Courts, hundreds and views	1512–13	11 pp. 2 atts.
1796	,, ,, ,, ,,	1563–4	3 mm.
1797	Courts and views	1564–5	3 mm.
1798	,, ,, ,,	1566–7	3 mm.
1801	,, ,, ,,	1569–70	3 mm.
1804	,, ,, ,,	1572–3	3 mm.
2019	,, ,, ,,	1573–4	3 mm.
1806	,, ,, ,,	1574–5	2 mm.
281	,, ,, ,,	1575–6	3 mm.
1808	,, ,, ,,	1576–7	3 mm.
1829	,, ,, ,,	1603 April	1 m.

CALEHILL   nos. 291–5

291	Hundreds and views [Courts at Charing]	1411–12	4 mm.
292	Same	1422–3	5 mm.
293	,,	1499–1500	11 pp. 2 atts.
294	,,	1510–11	18 pp. 2 atts.
295	,,	1514–15	5 mm.

CANTERBURY, ARCHBISHOP'S PALACE   nos. 1774–86

1774	Courts	1400–1	10 mm.
1775	,,	1401–2	8 mm.
1776	,,	1423–4	11 mm.
1777	,,	1436–7	10 mm.
1778	,,	1437–8	7 mm.
1779	,,	1578–9	9 mm.
1780	,,	1579–80	5 mm.
1781	,,	1585–6	1 m. 20 pp.
1782	,,	1597–8	6 mm.
1783	,,	1599–1602	4 mm.
1784	,,	1601–2	5 mm.
1785	,,	1603–4	6 mm.
1786	,,	1604–5	6 mm.

CANTERBURY, WESTGATE   nos. 1787–8

1787	Courts and views	1388–9	3 mm.
1788	,, ,, ,,	1412–13	2 mm.

CHARING, NEWLAND IN   no. 757

757	Courts	1354–7	1 m.

CODSHEATH   nos. 338–45

338	Hundred	1414	1 m.
340	,,	1429 October	1 m.
339	,,	1430 May	1 m.
341	,,	1431 October	1 m.
342	Hundreds [Courts at Bexley, Northfleet, Otford, Penshurst (hallmoot) and Wrotham, hundreds at Bexley, Somerden, Toltintrough and Wrotham, views at Cliffe, Crayford, Foots Cray, Halfley, Rust Hall in		

2

(342 *cont.*)	Speldhurst, Shipbourne and West Preston]	1520–1	13 mm. 1 att.
343	Same, but omitting courts and hundreds at Bexley, views at Rust Hall, and including views at Bexley	1534–5	6 mm.
344	Same as 342, but omitting courts at Bexley and Wrotham, hundreds at Bexley and Wrotham, and views at Rust Hall and Shipbourne, and including views at Bexley	1535–7	4 mm.
345	Same as 342, but omitting courts and hundreds at Bexley and Wrotham, views at Crayford, Foots Cray, Halfley and Rust Hall, and including views at Bexley	1536–7	5 mm.

CRAYFORD   no. 355

355	Views [Views at Cliffe, Foots Cray, Preston and Halfley]	1440–1	2 mm.

DOVER PRIORY   nos. 1998, 2003–5

2003	Courts [Courts at Brandred, Court Ash, Upper Deal, and Dudmanscombe in Buckland, Dover]	1728–91	363 pp. [book]
2004	Courts [Courts at Dudmanscombe]	1792–1835	315 pp. [book]
2005	Courts [Courts at Dudmanscombe and Brandred]	1840–92	331 pp. [book]
1998	Courts [Courts at Dudmanscombe]	1897–1937	223 pp. [book]

GILLINGHAM   nos. 462–6, 1791

462	Courts, hundreds and views	1480–1	1 m.
463	,, ,, ,, ,,	1502–3	1 m.
464	,, ,, ,, ,,	1505–6	2 mm.
465	,, ,, ,, ,,	1506–7	2 mm.
466	,, ,, ,, ,, [Courts, hundreds and views at Boughton and Teynham, hundreds and views at Calehill]	1547–8	5 mm.
1791	Courts, hundreds and views [Courts, hundreds and views at Boughton and Teynham]	1549–50	4 mm.

LYMINGE   nos. 617–18

617	Courts [Views at Loningborough (Lyminge) and Sibersnoth]	1449–50	2 mm.
618	Courts and views [Views at Oxney and Sibersnoth]	1465–6	3 mm.

MAIDSTONE   nos. 619–55

619	Courts [hallmoots and portmoots] and views	1382–3	5 mm.
620	,, ,, ,, ,, ,, ,,	1384–5	5 mm.
621	,, ,, ,, ,, ,, ,,	1385–6	5 mm.
622	,, ,, ,, ,, ,, ,,	1397–8	6 mm.
623	,, ,, ,, ,, ,, ,,	1402 October	2 mm.
624	,, ,, ,, ,, ,, ,,	1403–4	6 mm.
626	,, ,, ,, ,, ,, ,,	1404–5 Nov.–Jan.	1 m.

625	Courts [hallmoots and portmoots] and views						1405 Jan.–Aug.	5 mm.
627	,,	,,	,,	,,	,,	,,	1406–7	5 mm.
629	,,	,,	,,	,,	,,	,,	1408 October	1 m.
628	,,	,,	,,	,,	,,	,,	1408–9	4 mm.
630	,,	,,	,,	,,	,,	,,	1416–17 5 mm.	1 att.
631	,,	,,	,,	,,	,,	,,	1417–18	4 mm.
632	,,	,,	,,	,,	,,	,,	1420–1	5 mm.
633	,,	,,	,,	,,	,,	,,	1421–2	5 mm.
634	,,	,,	,,	,,	,,	,,	1434–5	4 mm.
635	,,	,,	,,	,,	,,	,,	1435–6	5 mm.
636	,,	,,	,,	,,	,,	,,	1437–8	4 mm.
637	,,	,,	,,	,,	,,	,,	1448–9	4 mm.
638	,,	,,	,,	,,	,,	,,	1464–5	2 mm.
639	,,	,,	,,	,,	,,	,,	1470–1	2 mm.
640	,,	,,	,,	,,	,,	,,	1480–1	2 mm.
641	,,	,,	,,	,,	,,	,,	1481–2	3 mm.
642	,,	,,	,,	,,	,,	,,	1482–3	2 mm.
643	,,	,,	,,	,,	,,	,,	1483–4	3 mm.
644	,,	,,	,,	,,	,,	,,		
	[Courts at Charing, courts, hundreds and views at Boughton, Calehill, Gillingham and Teynham]						1487–8	12 mm.
645	Courts [hallmoots and portmoots] and views						1497–8	3 mm.
646	,,	,,	,,	,,	,,	,,	1499–1500	3 mm.
647	,,	,,	,,	,,	,,	,,	1501–2	3 mm.
648	,,	,,	,,	,,	,,	,,	1504–5 15 pp.	5 atts. [draft with jury lists]
649	,,	,,	,,	,,	,,	,,	1505–6	5 mm.
650	,,	,,	,,	,,	,,	,,	1505–6 23 pp.	5 atts. [draft with jury lists]
651	,,	,,	,,	,,	,,	,,		
	[Courts at Charing, hundreds and views at Calehill]						1506–7	6 mm.
652	Courts [hallmoots and portmoots] and views						1508–9 16 pp.	2 atts. [draft]
653	,,	,,	,,	,,	,,	,,	1511–12 30 pp.	2 atts. [draft]
654	,,	,,	,,	,,	,,	,,		
	[Courts at Charing, courts, hundreds and views at Gillingham and Teynham, hundreds and views at Calehill]						1513–14	16 mm.
655	Courts [hallmoots and portmoots] and views						1521–2	4 mm.

NORTHFLEET   nos. 762–76, 1939

762	Courts [Hundreds and views at Toltintrough]	1314–15	6 mm.
763	Courts [Hundreds at Toltintrough]	1396–7	6 mm.
1939	Fragment containing presentments from Ifield and Luddesdown: part of a Toltintrough hundred roll	c. 1400	1 m. [incomplete]

764	Courts [Hundreds at Toltintrough]	1424–5	4 mm.
765	Courts	1425 May–June	1 m.
766	Courts [Hundreds at Toltintrough]	1449–50	3 mm.
767	,, ,, ,, ,,	1453–4	3 mm.
768	,, ,, ,, ,,	1456–7	3 mm.
769	,, ,, ,, ,,	1457–8	3 mm.
769A	,, ,, ,, ,,	1466–7	1 m.
770	,, ,, ,, ,,	1474–5	2 mm.
771	,, ,, ,, ,,	1476–7	2 mm.
772	,, ,, ,, ,,	1480–1	3 mm.
773	,, ,, ,, ,,	1486–7	3 mm.
774	,, ,, ,, ,,	1487–8	3 mm.
775	,, ,, ,, ,,	1488–9	3 mm.
776	,, ,, ,, ,,	1490–1	4 mm.

OTFORD   nos. 271, 475, 804–29

804	Courts [Hundreds at Bowbeach and Codsheath, view and hallmoot at Penshurst]	1388–9	18 mm.
807	Court	1403 December	1 m.
805	Courts [Hundreds at Codsheath, views at Bowbeach and Penshurst, and a hallmoot at Penshurst]	1403–4	15 mm.
806	Court	1404 September	1 m.
808	Courts [Hundreds at Codsheath, views at Bowbeach and Penshurst, and a hallmoot at Penshurst]	1405–6	19 mm.
809	Courts [Views at Bowbeach, Codsheath and Penshurst, and a hallmoot at Penshurst]	1410–11	11 mm.
811	Court	1414 October	1 m.
810	Courts	1414–15	4 mm.
271	Views at Bowbeach and Shipbourne [? part of 810]	1414–15	1 m.
812	Courts [Views at Earde in Crayford, Foots Cray and Halfley]	1415	9 mm.
814	Court	1417 October	2 mm. [incomplete]
813	Courts	1417–18	13 mm.
815	,,	1421–2	4 mm.
816	Court	1422 June	1 m.
817	,,	1424 October	1 m.
818	,,	1424 November	1 m.
819	,,	1424 December	1 m.
820	Courts [Hundreds at Codsheath, views at Bowbeach and Penshurst, and a hallmoot at Penshurst]	1426–7	18 mm.
821	Courts [Hundreds at Codsheath, views at Bowbeach, Earde in Crayford, Foots Cray, Halfley and Shipbourne, and a hallmoot at Penshurst]	1428–9	19 mm.
823	Court	1430 January	1 m.

822	Courts	1430 Feb.–April	3 mm.
824	Court	1430 July	1 m.
825	Courts [Hundreds at Codsheath, views at Bowbeach, Earde in Crayford, Foots Cray, Halfley, Northborough (? in Otford), Northfleet, Shipbourne and Styfford (? Stanford in Edenbridge), and a hallmoot at Penshurst]	1454–5	12 mm.
475	Views at Earde in Crayford, Foots Cray, Halfley and Northfleet	1455–6	1 m.
826	Courts [Hundreds at Bowbeach and Codsheath, views at Cliffe, Earde in Crayford, Foots Cray, Halfley, Preston in Shoreham, and Shipbourne, and hallmoots at Penshurst]	1462–3	12 mm.
827	Courts [Hundreds at Codsheath]	1497–8	6 mm.
828	Courts [Courts at Wrotham, hundreds at Codsheath, Somerden and Wrotham, and views at Shipbourne]	1500–1	8 mm.
829	Courts [Hundreds at Codsheath and Somerden, views at Shipbourne, and a hallmoot at Penshurst]	1501–2	6 mm.

| SOMERDEN | | no. 967 | |
| 967 | Hundred [Courts at Northfleet, Otford, and Penshurst (hallmoot), hundreds at Codsheath and Toltintrough, and views at Bexley, Cliffe, Crayford, Foots Cray, Halfley and Shipbourne] | 1556–7 | 8 mm. |

TEYNHAM		nos. 1039–40	
1039	Courts, hundreds and views	1448–9	3 mm.
1040	„ „ „ „	1501–2	2 mm.

WINGHAM		nos. 1121–2	
1121	Courts and hundreds	1387–8 Nov.–Jan.	1 m.
1122	Court and view of the King [during a vacancy of the see], and court and hundred	1486–7 Oct.–Mar.	1 m. [incomplete]

| WROTHAM | | no. 1138 | |
| 1138 | Courts and views | 1399–1400 | 6 mm. |

Middlesex

HARROW		nos. 477–8	
477	Courts and view	1507–8	5 pp. [draft]
478	„ „ „	1509–10	4 pp.

Surrey

CROYDON AND WADDON			nos. 1895–8, 1946–72, 1994–7, 2000–2, 2020–1, 2023, 2026	
2023	Courts and views [also a court book of Lambeth and other misc. *memoranda c.* 1580–1650]		1550–3	141 ff. [book]
1954	Courts and views		1585–1603	243 ff. [book]
1898	,, ,, ,,		1604–40	275 ff. [book]
2021	Estreats		1604–91	36 pp. [book]
1955	Courts and views	Croydon	1640–2 & 1660–91	478 pp. [book]
		Waddon	1648 & 1660–91	
1966	Estreats [Croydon only]		1660–1	2 mm.
1994	Courts and views		1660–81	46 mm.
1970	Estreats [Waddon only]		1665	1 m.
1971	,, ,, ,,		1666	2 mm.
1967	,, [Croydon ,,]		1666	2 mm.
1968	,,		1667	1 m.
1969	,, [Croydon only]		1669	1 m.
1972	,, [Waddon ,,]		1669	1 m.
1947	Courts and views		1682–1706	47 mm.
1956	,, ,, ,,		1692–1709	178 pp. [book]
1896	,, ,, ,,		1708–26	17 mm.
1957	,, ,, ,,		1710–26	199 pp. [book]
1946	Estreats [Lambeth also]		1724	1 m.
1948	Courts and views		1727–42	21 mm.
1958	,, ,, ,,		1727–64	463 pp. [book]
1897	,, ,, ,,		1743–52	12 mm.
1895	,, ,, ,,		1753–73	36 mm.
1959	,, ,, ,,		1765–73	158 pp. [book]
2000	Court fees [Lambeth also]		1772–1812	168 pp. [book]
1960	Courts and views		1774–95	359 pp. [book]
1949	,, ,, ,,		1786–9	6 mm.
1950	,, ,, ,,		1790–1804	26 mm.
1961	,, ,, ,,		1795–1817	317 pp. [book]
1951	,, ,, ,,		1805	2 mm.
1952	,, ,, ,,		1806	3 mm.
1953	,, ,, ,, [Waddon only]		1807	1 m.
1995	,, ,, ,, [Croydon ,,]		1807	2 mm.
2001	Court fees [Lambeth also]		1812–22	63 pp. [book]
1962	Courts and views		1818–32	567 pp. [book]
2002	Court fees [Lambeth also]		1822–28	241 pp. [book]
2020	Courts [Lambeth also]		1823–7	51 ff. [book: draft]
2026	,, ,, ,,		1823–8	60 ff. [book: draft]
1963	Courts		1832–43	507 pp. [book]

1964	Courts	1843–57	554 pp. [book]
1965	,,	1857–84	560 pp. [book]
1996	,,	1884–98	423 pp. [book]
1997	,,	1898–1950	260 pp. [book]

LAMBETH		nos. 1901–37, 1945–6, 1980–93, 2000–2, 2020, 2022–6	
1902	Courts and views	[1315–16]	4 mm.
1903	,, ,, ,, [and Lambeth Wick]	1385–6	3 mm.
1904	Courts and views	1422–35, 1436–42	38 mm.
1905	,, ,, ,,	1442–60	28 mm.
2022	,, ,, ,,	1488–91	8 ff. [book]
2023	,, ,, ,, [also a court book of Croydon and other misc. *memoranda c.* 1580–1650]	1550–3	141 ff. [book]
1906	Courts and views [and Lambeth Marsh]	1554–8	7 mm.
1901	Courts and views	1557–1604	210 ff. [book]
1980A	,, ,, ,,	1560–79	39 mm.
2025	Estreats	1585–1691	37 ff. [book]
1906A	Courts and views	1602–20	13 mm.
1912	,, ,, ,,	1604–34	177 ff. [book]
1913	,, ,, ,,	1635–83	216 ff. [book]
2024	,, ,, ,,	1648–60	24 ff. [book: copy]
1907	,, ,, ,,	1660–80	40 mm.
1933	Estreats	1660–1	2 mm.
1934	,,	1666	1 m.
1935	,,	1666	1 m.
1936	,,	1667	1 m.
1937	,,	1669	1 m.
1945	Quit rents	1669–1728	10 items
1908	Courts and views	1681–1707	62 mm.
1914	,, ,, ,,	1684–1709	393 pp. [book]
1909	,, ,, ,,	1708–26	24 mm.
1915	,, ,, ,,	1710–26	312 pp. [book]
1946	Estreats [Croydon and Waddon also]	1724	1 m.
1916	Courts and views	1727–50	368 pp. [book]
1980	,, ,, ,,	1727–53	45 mm.
1917	,, ,, ,,	1751–73	395 pp. [book]
1981	,, ,, ,,	1753–73	38 mm.
2000	Court fees [Croydon and Waddon also]	1772–1812	168 pp. [book]
1918	Courts and views	1774–96	359 pp. [book]
1982	,, ,, ,,	1786–90	5 mm.
1983	,, ,, ,,	1790–6	11 mm.
1910	,, ,, ,,	1797–1804	24 mm.
1919	,, ,, ,,	1797–1808	503 pp. [book]
1984	,, ,, ,,	1805–6	17 mm.
1911	,, ,, ,,	1807–8	24 mm.

1920	Courts and views	1809–18	634 pp. [book]
2001	Court fees [Croydon and Waddon also]	1812–22	63 pp. [book]
1921	Courts and views	1819–24	568 pp. [book]
2002	Court fees [Croydon and Waddon also]	1822–28	241 pp. [book]
2020	Courts [Croydon and Waddon also]	1823–7	51 ff. [book: draft]
2026	,, ,, ,, ,, ,,	1823–8	60 ff. [book: draft]
1922	Courts	1825–8	532 pp. [book]
1923	,,	1828–32	520 pp. [book]
1924	,,	1832–6	620 pp. [book]
1925	,,	1836–43	620 pp. [book]
1926	,,	1843–7	558 pp. [book]
1927	,,	1848–52	527 pp. [book]
1928	,,	1852–5	505 pp. [book]
1929	,,	1855–62	500 pp. [book]
1930	,,	1862–8	498 pp. [book]
1931	,,	1868–70	492 pp. [book]
1932	,,	1871–6	606 pp. [book]
1985	,,	1876–9	418 pp. [book]
1986	,,	1878–82	446 pp. [book]
1987	,,	1882–6	429 pp. [book]
1988	,,	1886–9	428 pp. [book]
1989	,,	1890–4	437 pp. [book]
1990	,,	1894–9	451 pp. [book]
1991	,,	1899–1904	468 pp. [book]
1992	,,	1905–20	462 pp. [book]
1993	,,	1919–41	264 pp. [book]

SOUTHWARK   no. 969

969	Courts and views	1504–11	6 mm.

Sussex

ALDWICK   nos. 143–86

143	Hundreds and views	1454–5	3 mm.
144	,, ,, ,,	1472–3	4 mm.
145	,, ,, ,,	1480–1	3 mm.
146	,, ,, ,,	1481–2	2 mm.
147	,, ,, ,,	1482–3	2 mm.
148	,, ,, ,,	1484–5 Mich.–Easter	2 mm.
149	,, ,, ,,	1485 Whitsun–Mich.	2 mm.
150	,, ,, ,,	1485–6	4 mm.
151	,, ,, ,,	1487–8	3 mm.
152	,, ,, ,,	1490	5 mm.
153	,, ,, ,,	1491–2	5 mm.
154	,, ,, ,,	1492–3	3 mm.
155	,, ,, ,,	1493–4	4 mm.
156	,, ,, ,,	1494–5	8 mm.
157	,, ,, ,,	1495–6	6 mm.

158	Hundreds and views			1496–7	4 mm
159	,,	,,	,,	1497–8	3 mm
160	,,	,,	,,	1498–9	4 mm
161	,,	,,	,,	1499–1500	5 mm
162	,,	,,	,,	1500–1	5 mm
163	,,	,,	,,	1501–2	5 mm
164	,,	,,	,,	1502–3	4 mm
165	,,	,,	,,	1504–5	5 mm
166	,,	,,	,,	1505–6	6 mm
167	,,	,,	,,	1506–7	8 mm
168	,,	,,	,,	1508–9	4 mm
169	,,	,,	,,	1510–11	4 mm
170	,,	,,	,,	1511–12	3 mm
171	,,	,,	,,	1513 June–July	1 m.
171A	,,	,,	,,	1513–14	4 mm
172	,,	,,	,,	1514–15	4 mm
173	,,	,,	,,	1515–16	4 mm
174	,,	,,	,,	1517–18	6 mm
175	,,	,,	,,	1518–19	4 mm
176	,,	,,	,,	1519–20	4 mm
177	,,	,,	,,	1520–1	4 mm
178	,,	,,	,,	1521–2	4 mm
179	,,	,,	,,	1524–5	7 mm
180	,,	,,	,,	1525–6	4 mm
181	,,	,,	,,	1528–9	5 mm
182	,,	,,	,,	1529–30	5 mm
183	,,	,,	,,	1533 May–Sept.	4 mm
184	,,	,,	,,	1533–4	6 mm
185	,,	,,	,,	1534–5	2 mm
186	,,	,,	,,	1557–8	7 mm

CHICHESTER, THE PALLANT				nos. 890–917	
890	Courts and views			1439–40 Mich.–April	1 m.
891	,,	,,	,,	1485–6	1 m.
892	,,	,,	,,	1489–90	1 m.
893	,,	,,	,,	1491–2	1 m.
894	,,	,,	,,	1493–4	1 m.
895	,,	,,	,,	1494–5	1 m.
896	,,	,,	,,	1503–4	1 m.
897	,,	,,	,,	1504–5	1 m.
898	,,	,,	,,	1506–7	1 m.
899	,,	,,	,,	1509–10	1 m.
900	,,	,,	,,	1511–12	1 m.
901	,,	,,	,,	1512–13	1 m.
902	,,	,,	,,	1513–14	1 m.
903	,,	,,	,,	1515–16	1 m.
904	,,	,,	,,	1516–17	1 m.
905	,,	,,	,,	1517–18	1 m.
906	,,	,,	,,	1518–19	1 m.
907	,,	,,	,,	1519–20	1 m.

908	Courts and views	1520–1	1 m.
909	,, ,, ,,	1521–2	1 m.
910	,, ,, ,,	1522–3	2 mm.
911	,, ,, ,,	1523–4	1 m.
912	,, ,, ,,	1524–5	1 m.
913	,, ,, ,,	1525–6	1 m.
914	,, ,, ,,	1527 Mich.	1 m.
915	,, ,, ,,	1528–9	1 m.
916	,, ,, ,,	1529–30	1 m.
917	,, ,, ,,	[1531] April	1 m.

LAVANT   nos. 599–606

599	Courts and views	1490–1 Oct–April	1 m.
600	,, ,, ,,	1505–6 Oct.–May	1 m.
601	,, ,, ,,	1506–7 Oct.–April	1 m.
602	,, ,, ,,	1513–14 Oct.–May	1 m.
603	,, ,, ,,	1525–6 Sept.–April	1 m.
604	,, ,, ,,	1528–9 Oct.–April	1 m.
605	,, ,, ,, [Courts and views at the Pallant and Tangmere, view at Aldwick]	1532 October	1 m.
606	Courts and views [Courts and views at the Pallant]	1534 September	1 m.

MALLING, SOUTH   nos. 681–8

681	Courts of Thomas de Useflete, canon [also account of income from the prebend]	1336–49	15 mm.
682	Courts of Thomas Boteler, canon	1384–6 Dec.–Jan.	2 mm.
683	,, ,, William Potyn, canon and precentor	1390 March–July	1 m.
684	,, ,, ,, ,, ,, ,, ,,	1390 Mich.–1392	2 mm.
685	,, ,, Robert Savage, ,, ,, ,,	1410 March–1411	2 mm.
686	,, ,, ,, ,, ,, ,, ,,	1411 Feb.–Oct.	1 m.
687	,, ,, ,, ,, ,, ,, ,,	1412 Jan.–May	1 m.
688	,, ,, ,, ,, ,, ,, ,,	1412 May–July	1 m.

MALLING, SOUTH, STONEHAM IN   no. 970

970	Hallmoot	1382 Mich.	1 m. [incomplete]

RINGMER   no. 942

942	Hundred [This hundred was carved out of the Arch-bishop's hundred at Loxfield in 1397: see *Place Names Sussex* ii, 352]	1407 March 29	1 m.

SLINDON   nos. 964–5

964	Courts and views	1485–6 Mich.–April	1 m.
965	,, ,, ,,	1527–8 Mich.–April	2 mm.

TANGMERE   nos. 995–1036

995	Courts and views	1437–8 Mich.–May	1 m.
996	,, ,, ,,	1470–1 Mich.–Easter	1 m.

997	Courts and views			1471–2 Mich.–Easter	1 m.
998	,,	,,	,,	1472–3 Mich.–Easter	1 m.
999	,,	,,	,,	1473–4 Mich.–May	1 m.
1000	,,	,,	,,	1481–2 Oct.–April	1 m.
1001	,,	,,	,,	1482–3 Oct.–Easter	1 m.
1002	,,	,,	,,	1488–9 Oct.–Easter	1 m.
1003	,,	,,	,,	1489–90 Oct.–April	1 m.
1004	,,	,,	,,	1490–1 Mich.–Easter	1 m.
1005	,,	,,	,,	1491–2 Mich.–Easter	1 m.
1006	,,	,,	,,	1492–3 Mich.–Easter	1 m.
1007	,,	,,	,,	1493–4 Mich.–April	2 mm.
1008	,,	,,	,,	1494–5 Oct.–Easter	1 m.
1009	,,	,,	,,	1496–7 Mich.–Easter	1 m.
1010	,,	,,	,,	1497–8 Mich.–Easter	1 m.
1011	,,	,,	,,	1498–9 Mich.–Easter	1 m.
1012	,,	,,	,,	1499–1500 Mich.–Easter	1 m.
1013	,,	,,	,,	1502–3 Mich.–Easter	1 m.
1014	,,	,,	,,	1503–4 Mich.–April	1 m.
1015	,,	,,	,,	1504–5 Mich.–Easter	1 m.
1016	,,	,,	,,	1507–8 Oct.–Easter	1 m.
1017	,,	,,	,,	1508–9 Mich.–May	1 m.
1018	,,	,,	,,	1509–10 Mich.–April	1 m.
1019	,,	,,	,,	1510–11 Mich.–May	1 m.
1020	,,	,,	,,	1511–12 Oct.–May	1 m.
1021	,,	,,	,,	1512–13 Mich.–April	1 m.
1022	,,	,,	,,	1514–15 Mich.–May	1 m.
1023	,,	,,	,,	1515–16 Mich.–April	1 m.
1024	,,	,,	,,	1516–17 Oct.–May	1 m.
1025	,,	,,	,,	1517–18 Oct.–April	1 m.
1026	,,	,,	,,	1518–19 Mich.–May	1 m.
1027	,,	,,	,,	1520–1 Mich.–July	1 m.
1028	,,	,,	,,	1523–4 Mich.–April	1 m.
1029	,,	,,	,,	[1524]–1525 Mich.–April	1 m.
1030	,,	,,	,,	1525–[1526] Mich.–April	1 m.
1031	,,	,,	,,	1526–7 Mich.–May	1 m.
1032	,,	,,	,,	1527–8 Mich.–April	1 m.
1033	,,	,,	,,	1529–30 Mich.–May	1 m.
1034	,,	,,	,,	1530–[1531] Mich.–April	1 m.
1035	Court and view [Courts and views at Slindon and Kirdford]			1535–6 Oct.–April	1 m.
1036	Courts and views [Courts, views and hundreds at Aldwick]			1536–7 Oct.–Oct.	3 mm.

TARRING, WEST				nos. 452, 1043–55A, 1059	
1043	Courts and views			1426–7	2 mm.
1044	,,	,,	,,	1427–8	1 m.
1045	,,	,,	,,	1428–9	1 m.
1059	Estreats of courts and views			1432 October	1 m.
1045A	Courts and views			1435–6	1 m.
452	,,	,,	,,	1472–3	2 mm.

1046	Courts and views	1473–4	1 m.
1047	,, ,, ,,	1487–8	2 mm.
1048	,, ,, ,,	1489–90	1 m.
1049	,, ,, ,,	1501–2	2 mm.
1050	,, ,, ,,	1503–4	2 mm.
1051	,, ,, ,,	1508–9	1 m.
1052	,, ,, ,, [Courts and views at Aldwick, Marlpost, Slindon and Tangmere]	1509–31, 1533–4, 1535–7, 1538–43, 1545–6	52 mm.
1053	Courts and views at Aldwick and Marlpost [? part of 1052]	1534–5	1 m.
1054	Courts and views at Kirdford, Marlpost and Slindon [? part of 1052]	1538–9	1 m.
1055	Courts and views [Courts and views at Marlpost]	1543–4	2 mm.
1055A	Courts and views [Courts and views at Marlpost]	1544–5	2 mm.

UCKFIELD		nos. 1078–84, 1899	
1078	Court	1382 November	2 mm.
1079	,,	1382/3 March	1 m.
			[incomplete]
1899	Courts	1386–7	12 mm.
1080	,,	1452 Feb.–Sept.	8 mm.
1081	,, [Courts at Lewes and Malling]	1466	15 mm. 1 att.
1082	,, [Hundreds at Lindfield, Loxfield and Ringmer, and a hallmoot at Stoneham in South Malling Without]	1487–9	21 mm.
1083	Courts [Hundreds at Lindfield, Loxfield and Ringmer, and a hallmoot at Stoneham]	1492–4	25 mm.
1084	Courts [Hundreds at Lindfield, Loxfield and Ringmer, and hallmoots at Stoneham]	1521–2	22 mm.

(2) Grouped properties for Kent
(including some estreats for Surrey)

		nos. 1162–75, 1786, 1789–90, 1792–5, 1799–1800, 1802–3, 1805, 1807, 1809–28, 1830–81, 2015	
1789	Views and courts at Deal Prebend, Down Barton in St Nicholas at Wade, Reculver, Westgate [Canterbury] and Wingham. [Hundreds and courts also at Wingham]	1488–9	10 mm.
1162	Same as above, except views and courts at Bishopstone in Reculver instead of Reculver	1511–12	15 mm.
1790	Ibid.	1534–5	7 mm.
1163	Same as 1789	1535–6	8 mm.
1164	Same as 1789 except views and courts at		

No.	Description	Date	Size
(1164 cont.)	Broomfield in Herne instead of Reculver. Also views and courts at Chislet, Northbourne and Petham	1545–6	18 mm
1165	Ibid.	1547–8	15 mm
1786	[? part of 1165] Courts at Combe in Newington, Hawkinge [Flegis Court in], Paddlesworth in Lyminge, and Satmar in Capel le Ferne	1547–8 Oct.–June	1 m.
1792	Same as 1164 except views and courts at Reculver instead of Broomfield	1552–3	12 mm
1793	Ibid.	1553–4	12 mm
1794	Views and courts at Chislet, Deal Prebend, Reculver and Westgate [Canterbury]	1560–1	6 mm
1166	Same as above. Also courts at Bekesbourne, Combe, Hawkinge [Flegis Court in], Pising in East Langdon, River, and Shelvingford in Hoath	1561–2	8 mm
2015	Views and courts as in 1794. Courts at Bekesbourne and Shelvingford	1562–3	6 mm
1795	Ibid.	1563–4	6 mm
1167	Same as 1166, but estreats and also a court at Sibertswold	1566–7	3 mm
1799	Ibid.	1567–8	4 mm
1800	Same as 2015	1568–9	2 mm
1802	Views and courts at Chislet, Reculver and Westgate [Canterbury]. Courts at Bekesbourne	1571 April	1 m.
1803	Same as 2015	1571–2	2 mm
1805	Views and courts at Chislet and Reculver. Courts at Bekesbourne, Hawkinge, Shelvingford and Sibertswold	1573–4	2 mm
1807	Views and courts at Chislet and Reculver. Courts at Shelvingford	1575 October	1 m.
1168	Same as 1167, but views and courts at Boughton also, and courts at Satmar but not at Bekesbourne	1578–9	3 mm
1809	Ibid.	1579–80	4 mm
1169	,,	1580–1	4 mm
1810	,,	1581–2	3 mm
1170	,,	1582–3	5 mm
1811	Same as 1168, but no courts at River or Sibertswold	1583–4	5 mm
1812	Same as 1168, but views and courts at Littlebourne also	1584–5	5 mm
1171	Same as 1168, but a court at Bekesbourne also	1585–6	7 mm
1813	Views and courts at Boughton, Chislet, Deal Prebend, Littlebourne, Reculver and Westgate [Canterbury]. Courts at Combe, Hawkinge, Shelvingford and four other places	1587–8	6 mm [mutilated

1814	Views and courts as above. Courts also at Pising, River, Satmar and Sibertswold	1588–9	8 mm.
1815	Same as 1814, but no court at Hawkinge	1589–90	8 mm.
1816	Views and courts as above. Court at Shelvingford only	1590–1	6 mm.
1817	Views and courts as above. Courts at Shelvingford, Combe, Hawkinge, River and Satmar	1591–2	6 mm.
1818	Views and courts at Boughton, Chislet, Littlebourne, Reculver and Westgate [Canterbury]. Court at Shelvingford	1592–3	6 mm.
1819	Views and courts as in 1813. Courts at Hawkinge, River, Satmar and Shelvingford	1593–4	7 mm.
1820	Same as 1818	1594–5	5 mm.
1821	Views and courts as in 1813. No separate courts	1595–6	3 mm.
1822	Ibid.	1596–7	3 mm.
1823	,,	1597–8	4 mm.
1824	,,	1598–9	4 mm.
1825	Same as 1816	1599–1600	4 mm.
1826	Views and courts as in 1813. No separate courts	1600–1	5 mm.
1827	Ibid.	1601–2	5 mm.
1172	Views and courts at Deal Prebend, Littlebourne, Reculver and Westgate [Canterbury]	1602 Mich.	1 m.
1828	Views and courts at Boughton, Chislet, Deal Prebend, [? Littlebourne], Reculver and Westgate [Canterbury]. Courts at Bekesbourne and Satmar	1602–3	2 mm. [much damaged]
1830	Views and courts as in 1813. No separate courts	1603–4	7 mm.
1831	Ibid.	1604–5	6 mm.
1173	,,	1607–8	5 mm.
1832	Views and courts as in 1813. Also court at Bekesbourne	1612–13	8 mm.
1174	Views and courts as in 1813. No separate courts	1615–16	6 mm.
1833	Ibid.	1627–8	7 mm.
1834	,,	1631–2	5 mm.
1175	,,	1639–40	8 mm.
1835	Views and courts at Boughton, Chislet, Littlebourne, Reculver and Westgate [Canterbury]	1660–1	5 mm.
1836	Views and courts as in 1813. Also a court at Shelvingford [and vouchers and estreats conc. archiepiscopal properties]	1661–2	7 mm.†
1837	Views and courts as in 1813. No separate courts	1662–3	7 mm.

† Indicates that the separate items have not been counted

15

1838	Views and courts as in 1813 [and vouchers]. No separate courts	1663-4	6 mm. †
1839	Views and courts at Boughton, Chislet, Deal Prebend, Littlebourne, Reculver and Westgate [Canterbury]. Courts at Combe, Hawkinge, Satmar and Sibertswold [and vouchers and estreats]	1664-5	10 mm. †
1840	Views and courts as in 1813 [and vouchers and estreats]. No separate courts	1665-6	7 mm. †
1841	Ibid.	1666-7	8 mm. †
1842	,,	1667-8	8 mm. †
1843	Same as 1832 [and vouchers and estreats]	1668-9	8 mm. †
1844	Views and courts as in 1813 [and vouchers and estreats]. No separate courts	1669-70	8 mm. †
1845	Same as 1836 [and vouchers and estreats]	1670-1	7 mm. †
1846	Same as 1839, but court also at Pising [and vouchers and estreats]	1671-2	9 mm. †
1847	Same as 1836 [and vouchers]	1672-3	7 mm. †
1848	Views and courts as in 1835 [and vouchers and estreats]. No separate courts	1673-4	6 mm. †
1849	Views and courts as in 1813 [and vouchers and estreats]. No separate courts	1674-5	7 mm. †
1850	Vouchers: Estreats for Boughton, Chislet, Deal Prebend, Littlebourne, Reculver, Westgate [Canterbury], and Lambeth, Croydon and Waddon [Surrey]	1675-6	50 items
1851	Views and courts as in 1813 [and vouchers and estreats]. No separate courts	1676-7	6 mm. †
1852	Ibid.	1677-8	6 mm. †
1853	,,	1678-9	7 mm. †
1854	,,	1679-80	6 mm. †
1855	,,	1680-1	6 mm. †
1856	Views and courts as in 1835 [and vouchers and estreats]. No separate courts	1681-2	7 mm. †
1857	Views and courts as in 1813 [and vouchers and estreats]. No separate courts	1682-3	6 mm. †
1858	Ibid.	1683-4	7 mm. †
1859	,,	1684-5	5 mm. †
1860	,, [and vouchers]	1685-6	5 mm. †
1861	,, [and vouchers and estreats]	1686-7	4 mm. †
1862	,,	1687-8	5 mm. †
1863	,, [and vouchers]	1688-9	10 mm. †
1864	Views and courts as in 1835 [and vouchers]. No separate courts	1690-1	4 mm. †
1865	Views and courts as in 1813 [and vouchers]. No separate courts	1691-2	9 mm. †
1866	Ibid.	1692-3	6 mm. †
1867	,,	1693-4	7 mm. †
1868	,,	1694-5	6 mm. †
1869	,,	1695-6	7 mm. †
1870	,,	1696-7	6 mm. †

871	Ibid.	1697–8	7 mm.†
872	,,	1698–9	6 mm.†
873	,,	1699–1700	6 mm.†
874	,,	1700–1	8 mm.†
875	,,	1701–2	6 mm.†
876	,,	1702–3	5 mm.†
877	,,	1703–4	6 mm.†
878	,,	1704–5	5 mm.†
879	,,	1705–6	5 mm.†
880	,,	1706–7	5 mm.†
881	,,	1708–9	6 mm.†

B. ACCOUNT ROLLS
(1) *Individual properties by counties: Bucks., Essex, Herts., Kent, Surrey and Sussex*

Bucks.

| HALTON | | no. 474 | |
| 474 | Reeve | 1306–7 | 2 mm. |

Essex

| HORNDON, WEST | | no. 1073 | |
| 1073 | Collector, stock keeper and farmers [Ingrave also]; accounts of repairs etc. and a receipt [Manor and advowson given to Archbishop Bourgchier: P. Morant, *The History . . . of Essex* i, London, 1768, 215] | 1478–9 | 4 pp. 4 atts. |

Herts.

| TRING | | no. 1077 | |
| 1077 | Bailiff | 1474–5 | 1 p. |

Kent

ALDINGTON		nos. 139–42	
139	Bedell, reeve, parker and farmer	1390–1	4 mm.
139A	Farmer	1441–2	1 m.
140	Serjeant	1443–4	2 mm.
141	,,	1444–5	2 mm.
142	Serjeant and bedell	1467–8	1 p.

| ASH, WINGHAM BARTON IN | | no. 1123 | |
| 1123 | Farmer | 1446–7 | 1 m. |

BEXLEY		nos. 234–46, 249–55	
234	Serjeant	1279	2 mm.
235	,,	1283–4	1 m.
236	Reeves, with court perquisites	1290–1	4 mm.
237	Reeve, ,, ,, ,,	1299–1300	3 mm.
238	,, ,, ,, ,,	1301–2	3 mm.
239	Reeve, with accounts for agistment	1302–3	3 mm.

C　　　　17

240	Reeve			1349–50	5 mm
241	Parker			1402–3	2 mm
242	,,			1403–4	1 m.
243	Parker and forester			1408–9	1 m.
244	Farmer			1410–11	1 m.
245	,,			1424–5	1 m.
246	Woodward and parker			1427–8	1 m.
249	,,	,,	,,	1429–30	1 m.
250	,,	,,	,,	1430–1	1 m.
251	,,	,,	,,	1437–8	1 m.
252	,,	,,	,,	1439–40	1 m.
253	Farmer			1443–4	1 m.
254	Woodward			1447–8	1 m.
255	Keeper			1489–90 or 1490–1	2 pp.

BISHOPSBOURNE   no. 288

288	Reeve	1443–5	1 m.

BISHOPSBOURNE, LANGHAM PARK IN   nos. 592–8

592	Parker	1397–8	1 m.
593	,,	1404–5	1 m.
594	,,	1408–9	1 m.
595	,,	1416–17	1 m.
596	,,	1420–1	1 m.
597	Parker and farmer	1424–5	1 m.
598	Parker	1429–30	1 m.

BOUGHTON UNDER BLEAN   no. 282

282	Reeve	1447–8	1 m.

BROOKLAND, WALLAND MARSH IN   MS. 951/1 [30]

MS. 951/1 [30]	Survey	1477 February 6	8 mm. [book]

CANTERBURY, ARCHBISHOP'S PALACE   no. 297

297	Keeper	1446–7	1 m.

CANTERBURY, EASTBRIDGE HOSPITAL   no. 296

296	Accounts	1349–51	9 mm.

CANTERBURY, WESTGATE   nos. 1102–5

1105	Rental and custumal [based on a survey of 1283–5, of which Cant. Cath. MS. E 24 is a 15th-cent. copy]	c. 1320	3 mm.
1102	Farmer	1431–2	1 m.
1103	,,	1443–4	1 m.
1104	Reeve	1447–8	2 mm.

CHARING   nos. 300–3, MSS. 790, 792

300	Keeper	1441–2	1 m.

301	Reeve	1443–4	2 mm.
302	Keeper	1446–7	1 m.
303	,,	1447–8	1 m.
MS. 790	Rental	c. 1484–5	33 ff.
			[book: copy]
MS. 792	,,	15th cent.	18 mm.
			[book: copy]

CLIFFE, BISHOP'S MARSH [BISHOPSMARSH] IN		nos. 257–69	
257	Farmer	1400–1	1 m.
258	,,	1408–9	1 m.
261	,,	1420–1	1 m.
259	,,	1423–4	1 m.
260	,,	1425–6	1 m.
262	,,	1429–30	1 m.
263	,,	1431–2	1 m.
264	,,	1433–4	1 m.
265	,,	1438–9	1 m.
266	,,	1443–4	1 m.
267	,,	1445–6	1 m.
268	,,	1447–8	1 m.
269	,,	1449–50	1 m.

CRANBROOK RECTORY		nos. 352–3	
352	Farmer	1445–6	1 m.
353	Bailiff	1471–2	1 p.

DEAL PREBEND		nos. 2036–46	
2043	Rental	1473–4	2 mm.
2044	,,	1569	5 mm.
2045	,,	1586	4 mm.
2046	Portion of a rental	late 16th cent.	2 mm.
2036	Rental	1807	26 ff. [book]
2037	,,	1808	25 ff. [book]
2038	,,	1809	26 ff. [book]
2039	,,	1811	43 ff. [book]
2040	,,	1813	35 ff. [book]
2041	,,	1815	44 ff. [book]
2042	Fines	1806–15	34 ff. [book]

FORD AND HERNE RECTORY		nos. 453, 1999, 2017	
1999	Keeper	1405–6	1 m.
			[incomplete]
453	Farmer	1443–4	1 m.
2017	[. . .]	c. 1460	4 mm.
			[incomplete]

GILLINGHAM		nos. 460–1, 1941,	
		MS. 1094[2]	
460	Reeve	1408–9	2 mm.

1941	Fragment of an account: Gillingham mentioned	*c.* 1430	1 m. [incomplete]
461	Reeve	1441–2	1 m.
MS. 1094[2]	Rental	1448–9	17 ff. [book]

IVYCHURCH, CHEYNE COURT IN		no. 326	
326	Farmer	1444–5	1 m.

IWADE, HERSING MARSH IN		nos. 480–93	
480	Farmer	1403–4	1 m.
481	,,	1423–4	1 m.
482	,,	1425–6	1 m.
483	,,	1427–8	1 m.
484	,,	1431–2	1 m.
485	,,	1432–3	1 m.
486	,,	1433–4	1 m.
487	,,	1435–6	1 m.
488	,,	1438–9	1 m.
489	,,	1440–1	1 m.
490	,,	1443–4	1 m.
491	,,	1444–5	1 m.
492	,,	1445–6	1 m.
493	,,	1447–8	1 m.

LEIGH, HILDENBOROUGH IN		no. 494	
494	Bedell	1388–9	1 m.

LITTLEBOURNE		no. 607	
607	Rental	1579	1 p.

LYMINGE		nos. 613–16	
613	Reeve	1414 Feb.–Mich.	2 mm.
614	Parker	1441–2	1 m.
615	Reeve	1443–4	2 mm.
616	,,	1446–7	2 mm.

MAIDSTONE		nos. 656–80, MS. 1025[1]	
656	Serjeant	1279–80 [or 1313–14]	2 mm.
657	Reeve [with estreats of courts]	1296–7	4 mm. 3 atts.
658	Serjeant [with estreats of courts]	1299–1300	2 mm. 2 atts.
659	Serjeant and reeve	1316–17	3 mm. 2 atts.
660	[Serjeant]	1317–18	2 mm.
661	Reeve	1318–19	2 mm.
662	[Serjeant]	*temp.* Edward II ʻ	2 mm.
663	Serjeant	*temp.* Edward II	4 mm.
664	,,	1331–2	2 mm.
665	,,	1335–6	3 mm.
666	Parker	1396–7	1 m.

667	Parker	1397–8	1 m.
668	Reeve	1398–9	3 mm.
669	Rental	*temp.* Richard II	14 mm.
670	Reeve	1408–9	5 mm.
671	,,	1409–10	3 mm.
672	Keeper and parker	1414–15	2 mm.
673	,, ,, ,,	1419–20	1 m.
674	Reeve	1423–4	2 mm.
675	,,	1430–1	2 mm.
676	Keeper	1433–4	1 m.
677	Reeve	1436–7	2 mm.
678	,,	1438–9	3 mm.
679	Keeper and parker	1442–3 Mich.–Apr. 12	1 m.
680	,, ,, ,,	1446–7	1 m.
MS. 1025[1]	Rental	*c.* 1509–10	43 ff. [book]

MAIDSTONE, OLDBOROUGH IN   no. 878

878	Farmer	1362–3	2 mm. 1 p.

NEWINGTON NEXT HYTHE, COMBE IN   no. 346

346	Rental	*c.* 1540	1 p.

NORTHBOURNE   no. 2064

2064	Copy of Collector's account [formerly a property of St Augustine's Abbey, Canterbury]	1538	1 m.

NORTHFLEET   nos. 777–803, 1940

777	Bailiff and reeve	[1303–4]	2 mm. 1 att.
778	Serjeant	1317–18	2 mm.
779	,,	1350–1	4 mm.
1940	,,	1359–60	2 mm.
780	,,	1363–4	3 mm.
781	,,	1364–5	4 mm.
782	,,	1366–7	3 mm.
783	Reeve	1368–9	2 mm.
784	Serjeant and reeve	1390–1	4 mm.
785	Farmer	1397 June–Sept.	1 m.
786	,,	1397–8	1 m.
787	Farmers, in the marshes of Little Harsyng and Bishopsmarsh in Cliffe, and Rowmarsh in Northfleet	1397–8	1 m.
788	Reeve	1398–9	2 mm.
789	Farmer	1399–1400	1 m.
790	Reeve	1399–1400	2 mm.
791	Farmer	1400–1 Sept.–June	1 m.
792	Serjeant	1401 June–Mich.	2 mm.
793	Reeve	1403–4	3 mm.
794	Serjeant	1408–9	3 mm.
795	Reeve	1409–10	2 mm.

796	Farmer	1424–5	1 m.
797	,,	1428–9	1 m.
798	Farmers	1435–6	1 m.
799	Reeve	1440–1	2 mm.
800	,,	1447–8	2 mm.
801	Farmer [rectory]	1447–8	1 m.
802	Reeve's petitions for allowances	temp. Edward IV	2 pp.
803	Account for building repairs at Northfleet parsonage	1504 December	1 p.

OTFORD		nos. 830–76	
831	Reeves, with pannage, heriots and reliefs	1296–7	5 mm. 1 att.
832	Serjeant	1315–16	3 mm.
833	,,	1322–3	4 mm.
830	,,	1323–4 [or 1288–9]	3 mm.
834	Reeve	1355–6	5 mm.
835	Serjeant	1382–3	4 mm.
836	[Serjeant]	1391–2	4 mm.
837	Parker	1399–1400	2 mm.
838	Serjeant	1402–3	4 mm.
839	Reeve	1404–5	4 mm.
840	Parker	1404–5	2 mm.
841	Serjeant	1405–6	1 m.
842 845A	Reeve	1406–7	3 mm.
843	Parker	1406–7	2 mm.
844	Reeve	1407–8	3 mm.
845	,,	1408–9	1 m.
846 846A	Serjeant	1410–11	4 mm.
847	Reeve	1410–11	3 mm.
848	Parker	1410–11	1 m.
849	Serjeant	1411–12	4 mm.
850	,,	1414 Feb.–Mich.	3 mm.
851	Parker	1414–15	1 m.
852	Reeve	1417–18	3 mm.
853	Serjeant	1418–19	3 mm.
854 854A	Reeve	1423–4	3 mm.
855	Parker	1424–5	1 m.
856	,,	1426–7	1 m.
857	Serjeant	1427–8	2 mm.
858	,,	1428–9	3 mm.
859	Reeve [Borgh of Otford]	1429–30	2 mm. 1 att.
860	Serjeant	1431–2	2 mm.
861	Reeve	1433–4	2 mm.
862	Parker	1433–4	1 m.
863	Serjeant	1437–8	2 mm.
864	Reeve [Borgh of Otford]	1438–9	1 m.
865	Serjeant	1439–40	2 mm.
866	Reeve [Borgh of Otford]	1439–40	2 mm.

867	Parker	1439–40	1 m.
868	Serjeant	1440–1	2 mm.
869	Reeve [Borgh of Otford]	1440–1	2 mm.
870	,, ,, ,, ,,	1443 June–Mich.	1 m.
871	Serjeant	1443–4	3 mm.
872	Reeve [Borgh of Otford]	1443–4	2 mm.
873	Parker	1443–4	1 m.
874	Reeve [Borgh of Otford]	1445–6	1 m.
875	Serjeant and keeper	1446–7	1 m.
876	Parker	1446–7	1 m.

OXNEY   no. 879

879	Collector	1444–5	1 m.

PETHAM   no. 918

918	Farmer	1445–6	1 m.

PETHAM, BUCKHOLT IN   no. 286

286	Forester, including deliveries of timber etc. to the palace at Canterbury for making 'les Hales' at Archbishop Stafford's institution	1443	1 m.

RECULVER   nos. 922–6

922	Reeve	1443 June–Mich.	1 m.	
923	,,	1443–4	2 mm.	
924	,,	1444–5	2 mm.	
925	,,	1445–6	2 mm.	
926	,,	1449–50	1 m.	1 att.

ST MARTIN'S NEW ROMNEY   no. 944

944	Collectors	1442–3	1 m.

ST NICHOLAS AT WADE RECTORY, THANET   no. 945

945	Farmer	1439–40	1 m.

SALTWOOD   nos. 946–8

946	Parker and farmer	1391–2	3 mm.
947	Reeve	1391–2	1 m. [incomplete]
948	Farmer	1444–5	1 m.

SEVENOAKS   no. 953

953	Reeve	1436–7	1 m.

SEVENOAKS, BRETONS MANOR IN   no. 285

285	Farmer [also receiver's account for Knole, Panthurst, Joces, and Riverhead in Sevenoaks]	1471–2	1 m.

SEVENOAKS, KNOLE, BRETONS, PANTHURST AND JOCES IN
no. 543, MS. 952[5]

543	Bailiffs and farmers	1466–7	2 pp. 2 atts.
MS. 952[5]	Parker of Knole's receipt	1523 December 31	1 p.

SEVENOAKS, WHITCLIFFE CHASE AND WOOD IN
no. 1111,
MS. 952[3]

1111	Forester	1406–7	1 m.
MS. 952[3]	Forester's receipt	1523 December 31	1 p.

SEVENOAKS WEALD
nos. 1087–90

1087	Reeve	1433–4		1 m.
1088	„	1435–6	1 m.	1 att.
1089	Collector	1445–6		1 m.
1090	„	1446–7		1 m.

SHOREHAM
nos. 955–6

955	Reeve	1432–3	1 m.
956	[Reeve]	c. 1430	1 m.
			[incomplete]

TEYNHAM
nos. 1037–8

1037	Serjeant	1393–4	1 m.
			[incomplete]
1038	Reeve	1443 June–Sept.	1 m.

THE LOWY OF TUNBRIDGE
no. 2066

2066	Receiver	1497 May–Sept.	4 pp.
	[Archbishop's during the minority of Edward, Duke of Buckingham]		

WESTBERE
no. 1474

1474	Terrier: Westbere, Hersden in Westbere, Ford Park and Herne mentioned	c. 1575	3 mm.
			[incomplete]

WROTHAM
nos. 1139–57, 2012, 2016, 2072

1139	Serjeant [with estreats of courts]	1309–10	6 mm.
2012	Reeve	c. 1355–6	2 mm.
1140	„	1356–7	5 mm.
1157	[Reeve]	c. 1375	2 mm.
1141	Rector and farmer	1397–8	1 m.
1142	Reeve and serjeant	[1399–1400 Mich.–Epiph.]	3 mm.
1143	Reeve	[1399–1400]	2 mm.
1143A	Farmer	[1400–1]	2 mm.
1144	Reeve	[1404–5]	2 mm.
2016	Account	[?1404–5]	3 mm.
1145	Serjeant	[1406–7]	3 mm.

146 146A	Reeve	[1408–9]	3 mm. 1 att.
147	Serjeant	[1410–11]	3 mm.
148	Reeve	1414 Feb.–Mich.	2 mm.
072	Farmer	1414 Feb.–Mich.	1 m.
149	Reeve	1415–16	2 mm.
150	,,	1416–17	2 mm.
151	,,	1417–18	2 mm.
152	Parker	1419–20	1 m.
153	Farmer	1419–20	1 m.
154	Parker	1420–1	1 m.
155	,,	1426–7	1 m.
156	Reeve	1433–4	2 mm.

Surrey

BURSTOW		no. 289	
289	Parker	1425–6	1 m.

CHEAM		nos. 309–23	
309	Farmer	1412–13	1 m.
310	,,	1424–5	1 m.
311	,,	1425–6	1 m.
312	,,	1426–7	1 m.
313	,,	1428–9	1 m.
314	,,	1430–1	1 m.
315	,,	1434–5	1 m.
316	,,	1436–7	1 m.
317	,,	1437–8	1 m.
318	,,	1438–9	1 m.
319	,,	1439–40	1 m.
320	,,	1440–1	1 m.
321	,,	1443–4	1 m.
322	,,	1444–5	1 m.
323	,,	1446–7	1 m.

CROYDON		nos. 356–61	
356	Reeve	1398–9	7 mm. 1 att.
357	Parker	1425–6	1 m.
358	Reeve	1427–8	3 mm.
359	Parker	1430–1	1 m.
360	Keeper	1432–3	1 m.
361	Reeve and parker	1454–5	1 m.

CROYDON, WADDON IN		no. 1085	
1085	Farmer	1440–1	1 m.

LAMBETH		nos. 545–77	
545	Reeve [also for Lambeth Wick]	1321–2	3 mm.
546	Serjeant [also for Lambeth Wick]	1349–50	3 mm. 3 atts.
547	Reeve	1391–2	1 m.
548	Reeves	1423–4	2 mm. 2 atts.

549	Keeper	1423–4	2 mm.
550	Reeve	1424–5	3 mm.
551	Keeper	1424–5	1 m.
552	Reeve	1425–6	2 mm.
553	,,	1426–7	2 mm.
554	,,	1427–8	2 mm.
555	Keeper	1428–9	1 m.
556	,,	1429–30	1 m.
557	Reeve	1430–1	2 mm.
558	Keeper	1430–1	1 m.
559	Reeves	1431–2	2 mm.
560	Keeper	1432–3	1 m.
561	Reeves	1433–4	2 mm.
562	Keeper	1433–4	2 mm. 2 atts.
563	,,	1434–5	1 m.
564	Reeve	1434–5	2 mm. 1 att.
565	Reeves	1436–7	2 mm. 1 att.
566	Keeper	1437–8	1 m.
567	Reeves	1437–8	1 m. 1 p.
568	Keeper	1438–9	1 m.
569	Reeve	1439–40	2 mm.
570	Keeper	1441–2	1 m.
571	Reeve	1443 June–Mich.	1 m.
572	,,	1443–4	1 m.
573	Keeper	1444–5	1 m.
574	Reeve	1444–5	1 m.
575	,,	1445–6	2 mm.
576	Keeper	1445–6	1 m.
577	Reeve	1446–7	1 m.

LAMBETH WICK   nos. 578–90

578	Farmer	1424–5	1 m.
579	,,	1426–7	2 mm.
580	,,	1430–1	1 m.
581	,,	1431–2	1 m.
582	,,	1432–3	1 m.
583	,,	1434–5	1 m.
584	,,	1435–6	1 m.
585	,,	1436–7	1 m.
586	,,	1438–9	1 m.
587	,,	1440–1	1 m.
588	,,	1441–2	1 m.
589	,,	1445–6	1 m.
590	,,	1446–7	1 m.

WIMBLEDON   nos. 1112–19

1112	Reeve	1389–90	3 mm.
1113	Farmer [and parkers of Burstow and Hampton]	1389–90	3 mm.
1114	Reeve and farmer [and parkers of Burstow and Hampton]	1390–1	8 mm. 1 att.

1115	Reeve	1402–3 [or 1403–4]	3 mm.
1116	Farmer	1429–30	1 m.
1117	,,	1430–1	1 m.
1118	,,	1434–5	1 m.
1119	Reeve	1436–7	3 mm.

Sussex

BERSTED		nos. 227–9	
227	Reeve	1382–3	2 mm.
228	Farmer	1437–8	1 m.
229	,,	1444–5	1 m.

FRAMFIELD		nos. 454–9	
454	Bedell	1420–1	4 mm.
455	,,	1423–4	3 mm.
456	,,	1424–5	3 mm.
457	,,	1435–6	2 mm. 1 att.
458	,,	1436–7	2 mm. 1 att.
459	Reeve	1437–8	2 mm. 2 atts.

MALLING, SOUTH		nos. 689–94, 2007	
2007	[. . .] account: Malling and Ranscombe mentioned	c. 1350	2 mm. [incomplete]
689	Keeper	1412–13	1 m.
690	,,	1426–7	2 mm.
690A	,,	1432–3	1 m.
691	,,	1436–7	1 m.
692	,,	1437–8	1 m.
693	,,	1439–40	1 m.
694	,,	1441–2	1 m.

| MALLING, SOUTH, RANSCOMBE IN | | no. 921 | |
| 921 | Farmer | 1440–1 | 1 m. |

MALLING, SOUTH, STONEHAM IN		nos. 971–2	
971	Serjeant	1392 March–Mich.	2 mm. [incomplete]
972	Stock keeper	1394–5	1 m.

MAYFIELD		nos. 695–719, 1900	
1900	Bedell	1388–9	2 mm. 2 atts.
695	Serjeant of the rectory	1394–5	3 mm.
696	Keeper of the rectory	1412–13	3 mm.
697	Farmer	1423–4	1 m.
698	Seller of grain of the rectory	1424–5	2 mm.
699	Bedell	1425–6	3 mm.
700	,,	1427–8	3 mm.
701	Farmer	1431–2	1 m. 1 att.
702	,,	1432–3	2 mm.
703	Bedell	1434–5	2 mm. 1 att.

704	Bedell	1435–6	2 mm.
705	Farmer	1435–6	1 m.
706	,,	1437–8	1 m.
707	,,	1438–9	1 m.
708	Parker	1438–9	1 m.
709	Bedell	1440–1	2 mm.
710	Farmer	1441–2	1 m.
711	Bedell	1441–2	2 mm.
712	Keeper of the rectory	1443–4	1 m.
713	,, ,, ,, ,,	1444–5	1 m.
714	Parker and keeper of the manor	1445–6	1 m.
715	Bedell	1449–50	1 m. 2 atts.
716	Farmer of the rectory	1449–50	1 m.
717	Parker	1449–50	1 m.
718	Bedells	*temp.* Edward IV	1 m. [incomplete]
719	,,	1492	1 p. [incomplete]

PAGHAM		nos. 880–9, 1428	
880	Stock keeper	1425–6	2 mm.
881	Chamberlain	1425–6	2 mm.
882	,,	1426–7	2 mm.
883	,,	1427–8	3 mm. 1 att.
884	,,	1430–1	2 mm.
1428	[. . .]	[1431–2]	3 mm.
885	Chamberlain	1435–6	2 mm.
886	,,	1443–4	2 mm.
887	,,	1444–5	2 mm.
888	,,	1446–7	2 mm.
889	,,	*c.* 1485–6	1 m.

PAGHAM, NYETIMBER IN		nos. 758–61	
758	Grainseller	1426–7	2 mm. 1 att.
759	Farmer	1426–7	1 m.
760	Collector	1438–9	1 m.
761	Rental of rents and services	1529 Mich.	1 m.

RINGMER		nos. 927–41	
927	Chamberlain	1387–8	3 mm.
928	,, [and forester of South Malling]	1391–2	4 mm.
929	Bedell and rent collector	1393–4	1 m. [incomplete]
930	Chamberlain	1425–6	4 mm.
931	,,	1427–8	5 mm.
932	,,	1432–3	3 mm.
933	,,	1435–6	2 mm.
934	Parker	1435–6	1 m.
934A	,,	1436–7	1 m.
935	,,	1437–8	1 m.
936	,,	1438–9	1 m.

937	Chamberlain	1439–40	2 mm.
938	Parker	1441–2	1 m.
939	Chamberlain	1443–4	3 mm.
940	Parker	1443–4	1 m.
941	Chamberlain	1449–50	2 mm.

SHRIPNEY		nos. 957–63	
957	Farmers	1394–5	1 m.
958	Farmer	1423–4	2 mm.
959	Reeve	1425–6	3 mm.
960	Collector	1432–3	1 m.
961	Farmer	1434–5	1 m.
962	Collector	1443–4	1 m.
963	Farmer	1447–8	1 m.

SLINDON		no. 966	
966	Wood accounts, headed "Slyndon Wode sale"	c. 1530	1 p.

TANGMERE		nos. 976–94	
976	Reeve	1382–3	4 mm.
977	,,	1385–6	2 mm.
978	Farmer	1424–5	2 mm.
979	Grainseller	1424–5	1 m.
980	Farmer	1425–6	1 m.
981	,,	1427–8	1 m.
982	,,	1430–1	1 m.
983	,,	1431–2	1 m.
984	,,	1432–3	1 m.
985	,,	1436–7	1 m.
986	,,	1439–40	1 m.
987	,,	1440–1	1 m.
988	,,	1441–2	1 m.
989	,,	1443 June–Mich.	1 m.
990	,,	1443–4	1 m.
991	,,	1444–5	1 m.
992	,,	1445–6	1 m.
993	,,	1446–7	1 m.
994	,,	1447–8	1 m.

TARRING, WEST		nos. 1056–8, 1060–71	
1056	Farmer and collector	1423–4	1 m.
1057	,, ,, ,,	1425–6	1 m.
1058	,, ,, ,,	1427–8	1 m.
1060	Farmer	1432–3	1 m.
1061	,,	1433–4	1 m.
1062	,,	1434–5	1 m.
1063	,,	1436–7	1 m.
1064	,,	1437–8	1 m.
1065	,,	1438–9	1 m.
1066	,,	1439–40	1 m.

1067	Farmer	1440–1	1 m.
1068	,,	1444–5	1 m.
1069	,,	1445–6	1 m.
1070	,,	1446–7	1 m.
1071	,,	1447–8	1 m.

WADHURST   no. 1086

| 1086 | Farmer | 1387–8 | 1 m. |

[Custumals of the Archbishop's manors in Sussex have been edited by B. C. Redwood and A. E. Wilson, *Sussex Record Society* lvii, 1958]

(2) *Household Account*

no. 1973

1973 Archbishop Thomas Bourgchier   1459 5–31 Oct.   5 pp.
[cf. W. A. M. no. 9222: an early Canterbury   [incomplete]
household roll of Archbishop John Stratford, dated 1343]

(3) *Valor*

no. 2063

2063 Valor by bailiwicks [Aldington, Croydon, Maidstone, South Malling, Otford, Pagham and Wingham]   1422   8 mm.

(4) *Rental and Survey*

no. 2068

2068 Survey* of, and rents etc. from Aldington, Bexley, Bishopsbourne, Boughton, Charing, Deal, Gillingham, Lydd, Lyminge, Maidstone, Newchurch, Newenden, Northfleet, Otford, Oxney, Petham, Reculver, Romney, St Martin's *al.* Caldicote in Canterbury, St Martin's New Romney, Saltwood, Shirley Moor in Woodchurch, North Stour, Teynham, Thanet, Weald in Aldington bailiwick, Westgate [Canterbury], Willop in Burmarsh, Wingham, Wingham Barton in Ash, and Wrotham [all in Kent], Harrow, Hayes, and Wood Hall in Pinner [all in Middlesex], Cheam, Croydon, Lambeth, Mortlake and Wimbledon [all in Surrey], and Aldwick, Bersted, Lavant, South Malling, Mayfield, Nyetimber in Pagham, Pagham, Ranscombe in South Malling, Shripney, Slindon, Stone-

*[An abbreviated form of the 1283–5 survey of which Cant. Cath. MS. E 24 is a 15th-cent. copy]

30

(2068   ham in South Malling, Tangmere and
cont.)   Tarring [all in Sussex]:
          includes also a copy of the bailiff's oath
          [in French]; a list of the denns of the
          Archbishopric in the Weald, and a copy
          of the Custom of Kent   c. 1285   9 mm. 1 att.

(5) Ministers' Accounts: Various manors
no. 1193

1193   Accounts for Bexley, Brasted, Northfleet and
        Tunbridge Wells [Kent], Harrow on the
        Hill and Hayes [Middlesex], and Croydon,
        Lambeth and Wimbledon [incl. Burstow
        and Mortlake] [Surrey]   1236–7   3 mm.
                                                          [incomplete]

        [on the date see C. H. Lawrence, St. Ed-
        mund Rich, Oxford, 1960, 139 n. 4]

(6) Ministers' Accounts by bailiwicks

BAILIWICK OF ALDINGTON   nos. 1193A–1210A,
                                           1427, 2018

1427   Fragment [? part of an Aldington bailiwick
        roll]   [c. 1300–25]   1 m.
1193A   Accounts of various ministers for Aldington,
        Bourne [al. Bishopsbourne], Buckholt in
        Petham, Cheyne Court in Ivychurch,
        Cranbrook rectory, Langham Park in
        Bishopsbourne, Lydd, Lyminge, New-
        church, North Stour, Oxney, Petham, St
        Martin's New Romney, Saltwood, Shirley
        Moor in Woodchurch, Sibersnoth in Orle-
        stone, Weald, and Willop in Burmarsh   1455–6   15 mm.
1194   Same as above, omitting Shirley Moor and
        Weald   1465–6   14 mm.
1195   Ibid.   1466–7   14 mm.
1196   Same as 1193A   1471–2   12 mm.
1197   Draft of the above   1471–2   12 pp.
1198   Same as 1193A   1474–5   11 mm.
2018   Similar   1475–6   10 mm. 1 p.
                                                          [mutilated]
1199   Same as 1193A, but omitting Shirley Moor 1477–8   13 mm.
1200   Same as 1193A, but omitting Shirley Moor,
        Newchurch and Weald, and including
        Cheyne Marsh and Becard   1484–5   16 mm.
1201   Same as 1193A, but including Cheyne Marsh
        and Becard, and omitting Sibersnoth   1496–7   16 mm.
1202   Same as 1193A, but omitting Buckholt, and
        including Cheyne Marsh and Becard   1501–2   10 mm.
1203   Same as 1193A, but omitting Buckholt, Shir-

(1203 *cont.*)	ley Moor and Sibersnoth, and including Cheyne Marsh and Becard	1504–5	15 mm.
1204	Same as above, but also omitting Langham Park	1506–7	13 mm.
1205	Same as 1193A, but omitting Shirley Moor and Sibersnoth, and including Cheyne Marsh and Becard	1507–8	13 mm.
1206	Vouchers for these properties	1513–14	32 items
1207	Same as 1193A, but omitting Langham Park and Sibersnoth, and including Cheyne Marsh, Becard and Newenden	1516–17	13 mm.
1208	Same as 1193A, but omitting Buckholt, and including Cheyne Marsh and Becard	1525–6	11 mm.
1209	Same as 1193A, but omitting Shirley Moor, and including Cheyne Marsh, Becard and Newenden	1529–30	11 mm.
1210	Same as 1193A, but omitting Cranbrook, Petham and Shirley Moor, and including Cheyne Marsh, Becard and Newenden	1532–3	6 mm.
1210A	Same as 1193A, but omitting Buckholt, and including Cheyne Marsh, Becard and Newenden	1537–8	13 mm.

BAILIWICK OF BOUGHTON no. 1211

1211	Accounts of various ministers for Boughton, Gillingham and Teynham	1547–8	4 mm.

BAILIWICK OF CHARING no. 1212

1212	Accounts of various ministers for Charing, Gillingham and Teynham	1544–5	7 mm.

BAILIWICK OF CROYDON nos. 1213–21

1213	Accounts of various ministers for Burstow, Cheam, Croydon, Lambeth, Lambeth Wick, Mortlake, Waddon in Croydon, and Wimbledon [Surrey], for Harrow, Hayes, Headstone in Pinner, Pinner, Sudbury, Wood Hall in Pinner [Middlesex], and for Tring [Herts.]	1458–9	12 pp.
1214	Ibid.	1466–7	12 pp.
1215	Same as above, but omitting Hayes, Headstone, Pinner, Wood Hall and Tring	1473–4	8 pp.
1216	Same as 1213	1482–3	11 pp. 2 atts.
1217	,, ,, ,, but omitting Harrow, Hayes, Headstone, Sudbury and Wood Hall	1485–6	7 mm.
1218	Same as 1213	1488–9	12 pp.
1219	Ibid.	1489–90	11 mm.
1220	Same as above, but omitting Mortlake	1503–4	9 pp.
1221	Same as 1213, but omitting Burstow, Cheam, Mortlake and Wimbledon [Surrey], and Hayes [Middlesex]	1543–4	9 mm.

AILIWICK OF MAIDSTONE   nos. 1222–39, 1429

222	Various accounts for Boughton, Charing, Gillingham and Teynham	c. 1350	4 mm.
429	Fragment [? part of a Maidstone bailiwick roll]	[1441–2]	2 mm.
223	Accounts of various ministers for Boughton, Charing, Maidstone and Teynham	1457–8	6 pp. 1 att.
224	Same as above, but with Gillingham and Oakenpole in Doddington also	1459–60	9 mm.
225	Same as above, but omitting Oakenpole	1460–1	7 mm.
226	Same as 1224	1461–2	9 mm.
227	„ „ 1225	1463–4	9 pp.
228	„ „ 1224	1464–5	8 mm.
229	„ „ 1225. [Also receiver's account for the whole bailiwick]	1467–8	9 mm.
230	Same as 1225, but with Oldborough in Maidstone also	1473–4	7 mm.
231	Ibid.	1493–4	11 pp.
232	Vouchers relating to places in the bailiwick	1494–5	30 items
233	„ „ „ „ „ „ „	1499–1500	24 items
234	Accounts of various ministers for Charing, Gillingham, Maidstone [and Oldborough in], Oakenpole and Teynham	1500–1	10 mm.
235	Same as above, but omitting Oakenpole, and including Boughton	1506–7	8 mm.
236	Vouchers	1508–9	40 items
237	„	1511–12	30 items
238	„	1512–13	20 items
239	„	1522–3	42 items

BAILIWICK OF MALLING, SOUTH   nos. 1301–34

301	Accounts for Stoneham in South Malling, and Tarring	1348 Aug.–Nov.	5 mm.
302	Accounts of various ministers for Broyle forest in Ringmer, Framfield, Frankham Park in Wadhurst, Mayfield, More Park in Ringmer, Plashett Park in Ringmer, Ranscombe in South Malling, Ringmer, South Malling, Southerham and Stoneham [both in South Malling], and Wadhurst	1456–7	9 mm.
303	Same as above, but not including Frankham and Wadhurst	1458–9	8 pp.
304	Same as 1302	1461–2	6 mm.
305	Ibid.	1462–3	6 mm.
306	Same as 1302, but omitting Wadhurst	1465–6	8 pp.
307	Same as 1302, but omitting Ranscombe and Southerham	1468–9	7 pp.
308	Same as 1302, but omitting Broyle forest, Frankham, Southerham and Wadhurst	1471–2	6 mm.
309	Same as 1302	1478–9	8 pp.
310	Fragment: no heading	1479–80	2 mm.

D

33

1311	Same as 1302, but omitting South Malling	1485–6	8 mm
1312	Ibid.	1488–9	9 mm
1313	,,	1489–90	9 pp. [summary]
1314	Same as 1311, but not including Mayfield	1490–1	8 pp. [summary]
1315	Same as 1311	1491–2	9 mm
1316	Ibid.	1492–3	10 pp.
1317	,,	1493–4	10 pp.
1318	,,	1501–2	7 pp.
1319	Same as 1311, but not including Framfield, More Park and Plashett Park	1502–3	5 pp.
1320	Vouchers relating to places in the bailiwick	1505–6	32 items
1321	Same as 1311	1507–8	11 mm
1322	Vouchers	1509–10	32 items
1323	Same as 1311, but omitting Southerham and Wadhurst	1516–17	8 mm
1324	Same as 1311	1518–19	7 mm
1325	Same as 1311, but omitting Broyle forest, Mayfield, More Park and Frankham Park	[1519–20]	2 mm
1326	Same as 1311, but omitting Broyle forest	1520–1	8 mm
1327	Debit accounts for Broyle forest, Framfield, Frankham Park, Mayfield, More Park, Plashett Park, Ranscombe, Ringmer, Southerham, Stoneham and Wadhurst, plus a receipt and several vouchers	1517–22	11 pp. 4 atts.
1328	Accounts of various ministers for the same places as above	1530–1	10 mm
1329	Ibid.	1532–3	6 mm
1330	,,	1533–4	9 mm
1331	Same as above, but omitting Southerham	1539–40	10 mm
1332	Same as above, but omitting Southerham, Mayfield and Wadhurst	1540–1	8 mm
1333	Same as above, but omitting Southerham, Broyle forest and More Park [heading only]	1543–4	12 mm
1334	Same as 1333 but also omitting Plashett Park	1545–6	7 mm

BAILIWICK OF OTFORD   nos. 1240–59

1240	Accounts of various ministers for Bexley, Bishop's Marsh in Cliffe, Chevening, Hersing Marsh in Cliffe, Northfleet, Otford, Sevenoaks, Sevenoaks Weald, Shoreham, Whitcliffe Chase and Wood in Sevenoaks, and Wrotham. Also receiver's account for the whole bailiwick	1453–4	14 mm.
1241	Ibid.	1454–5	13 mm.
1242	Accounts of various ministers for Chevening, Northfleet, Otford, Sevenoaks, Shoreham, [? Weald] and Wrotham. No receiver's account	1458–9	8 pp. [mutilated]

34

1243	Same as 1240	1460–1	10 mm.
1244	,, ,, ,, , but no accounts for Bishop's Marsh and Hersing Marsh, and no receiver's account	1468–9	10 pp.
1245	Same as 1240	1469–70	12 mm.
1246	Same as 1244, but with a receiver's account for the bailiwick	1473–4	10 pp.
1247	Vouchers relating to places in the bailiwick	1484–5	15 items
1248	Same as 1240, but including Knole [in Sevenoaks] also	1486–7	14 pp.
1249	Vouchers	1487	34 items
1250	Same as 1240, but no receiver's account	1493–4	14 pp.
1251	Ibid.	1504–5	12 pp. 1 att.
1252	Accounts of various ministers for Bexley, Chevening, Hersing Marsh, Knole, Northfleet, Otford, Sevenoaks, Sevenoaks Weald, Shoreham, Whitcliffe and Wrotham	1505–6	16 mm.
1253	Vouchers	1507	26 items
1254	,,	1510	20 items
1255	,,	1512	16 items
1256	,,	1514–15	15 items
1257	,,	1516–17, 1517–18	32 items
1258	Same as 1252	1521–2	10 mm.
1259	Vouchers	1522–3	9 items

BAILIWICK OF PAGHAM   nos.1260–1300, 2069

1260	Accounts of various ministers for Aldwick, Bersted, Lavant, Nyetimber, Pagham, Shripney, Slindon, Tangmere and Tarring	1450–1	12 mm.
1261	Same as above, but also including Slindon Park and Chase	1453–4	11 mm.
1262	Same as 1260	1455–6	10 mm.
1263	,, ,, ,, , but also including Slindon Park	1457–8	7 mm.
1264	Ibid.	1458–9	6 mm.
1265	Same as above, but omitting Tarring	1461–2	6 mm.
1266	Same as 1263, but omitting Shripney	1465–6	6 mm.
1267	Same as 1263	1467–8	6 mm.
1268	Ibid.	1468–9	6 mm.
1269	Same as 1261	1470–1	5 mm.
1270	Ibid.	1471–2	5 pp. [draft]
1271	,,	1472–3	5 mm.
1272	,,	1474–5	6 pp. [summary]
1273	,,	1474–5	5 mm.
1274	,,	1476–7	5 mm.
1275	Same as 1260	1476–7	5 pp. [summary]
1276	Same as 1261	1477–8	5 mm.
1277	Ibid.	1478–9	5 mm.
1278	,,	1479–80	6 pp.

1279	Same as 1260, but omitting Slindon and Tarring	1480–1	3 mm.
1280	Same as 1261	1483–4	5 mm.
1281	Same as 1260, but omitting Slindon [one membrane cut]	1484–5	7 mm.
2069	Cover only: roll lacking	1488–9	1 m.
1282	Same as 1260, but also including Withering port	1492–3	7 pp. 1 att. [summary]
1283	Ibid.	1493–4	7 mm.
1284	,,	1493–4	7 pp. [summary]
1285	,,	1494–5	7 mm.
1286	,,	1494–5	8 pp. [summary]
1287	Same as 1282, but omitting Tangmere, and the entry for the port of Withering not completed	1499–1500	7 mm.
1288	Same as 1260, but omitting Nyetimber	1501–2	4 pp. [summary]
1289	Same as 1260	1503–4	7 mm.
1290	,, ,, ,, , but with title for Withering port [entry not completed]	1504–5	7 mm.
1291	Vouchers relating to places in the bailiwick	1504–5	36 items
1292	Same as 1260, but the heading for Shripney lacking	1516–17	5 mm.
1293	Same as 1260	1517–18	4 mm.
1294	Ibid.	1518–19	4 mm.
1295	Same as 1290, but no entry for Shripney	1521–2	5 mm.
1296	Vouchers	1524	17 items
1297	,,	1528	20 items
1298	Same as 1260 [several pieces cut out]	1528–9	5 mm.
1299	Same as 1260, but with receiver's account for the bailiwick	1533–4	6 mm.
1300	Accounts of various ministers for Nyetimber, Pagham, Slindon, Tangmere and Tarring	1536–7	5 mm.

BAILIWICK OF WINGHAM   nos. 1335–42

1335	Accounts of various ministers for Curlswood in Nonington, Deal, Reculver, St Nicholas at Wade, Stourmouth, Westgate [Canterbury], Wingham, and Wingham Barton in Ash, and voucher and *memorandum*	1463–4	6 pp. 2 atts.
1336	Vouchers relating to Aldington and Wingham bailiwicks	1502–3	33 items
1337	Same as 1335, but also including Canterbury Palace, Ford Park in Herne, Ford and Herne rectory, and North and South Bishopsden Woods in Dunkirk	1536–7	7 mm.
1338	*Bailiwicks of Northbourne and Westwell.* Accounts of various ministers for Ashley		

1338 cont.)	in Northbourne rectory, Bekesbourne, Chislet, Coldred, Grauntesley Marsh [unid.], Hull manor with Sholden rectory, Northbourne manor and rectory, Ripple, Shelvingford [in the parishes of Reculver, Chislet, Herne and Westbere], and West-well manor and rectory	1544–5	8 mm.
339	Same as 1335, but also including Buckholt, Ford and Herne rectory, Petham, and Shirley Moor in Woodchurch	1546–7	9 mm.
340	Ibid.	1547–8	7 mm.
341	Same as 1338, but omitting Ripple, and including Beauxfield [Whitfield] rectory	1547–8	7 mm.
342	*Bailiwick of Wingham, Chislet and West Langdon.* Same as 1335, but also including Buckholt, and Ford and Herne rectory: same as 1338, but also including Beauxfield rectory: West Langdon: Alkham, Blackwose in Saltwood, Combe in Newington, Dover, Enbrook in Cheriton, Hawkinge, Paddlesworth in Lyminge, Pising in East Langdon, Postling, Portslade rectory [Sussex], Satmar in Capel le Ferne, and Sibertswold	1549–50	22 mm.

(7) Receivers' Accounts by bailiwicks

nos. 285, 1229, 1240,
1241, 1243, 1245,
1246, 1248, 1299,
1343–77, 1885, 2008,
2010, 2014, 2051

1343	Bailiwicks of Croydon and Otford	1424–5	3 mm.
1344	Bailiwicks of Croydon, Otford, Pagham and South Malling, and receipt	1437–8	2 mm. 1 att.
1345	Bailiwicks of Croydon and Pagham	[1442–3]	2 mm. [incomplete]
1240	Bailiwick of Otford [also accounts of various ministers]	1453–4	14 mm.
1241	Ibid.	1454–5	13 mm.
1346	Bailiwicks of Aldington, Maidstone, Otford and Wingham	1459–60	2 mm.
1243	Bailiwick of Otford [also accounts of various ministers]	1460–1	10 mm.
1347	Bailiwicks of Aldington, Maidstone, Otford and Wingham	1464–5	3 mm.
1347A	Bailiwicks of Croydon and South Malling	1466–7	3 mm.
1229	Bailiwick of Maidstone [also accounts of various ministers]	1467–8	9 mm.
2051	Bailiwicks of Croydon, Pagham and South Malling	1453–4	2 mm.

37

1348	Bailiwick of Otford	1467–8	2 pp.
1245	„ „ „ [also accounts of various ministers]	1469–70	12 mm.
285	Bailiwick of Otford [Knole, Panthurst, Joces, and Riverhead in Sevenoaks] [also farmer's account of Bretons in Sevenoaks]	1470–2	1 m.
1349	Bailiwicks of Croydon, Pagham and South Malling	[1472–3]	5 pp. [incomplete]
1246	Bailiwick of Otford [also accounts of various ministers]	1473–4	10 pp.
1350	Bailiwicks of Croydon, Pagham and South Malling	1478–9	3 mm.
1351	Bailiwicks of Aldington and Maidstone	1479–80	2 mm.
1248	Bailiwick of Otford [also accounts of various ministers]	1486–7	14 pp.
1352	Bailiwicks of Croydon, Pagham and South Malling, and 2 receipts	1490–1	2 mm. 2 atts.
1353	Bailiwick of Pagham and 2 receipts	1492–3	1 m. 2 atts.
1354	Bailiwick of Otford and 2 receipts	1493–4	2 mm. 2 atts.
1355	Ibid.	1494–5	2 mm. 2 atts. [incomplete]
1356	Bailiwick of Pagham	1494–5	1 m. [incomplete]
1357	Bailiwick of Otford and 2 receipts	1495–6	3 mm. 2 atts.
1358	Bailiwicks of Aldington and Wingham	1495–6	8 pp. [summary]
2010	Bailiwick of Otford	[1496–7]	3 pp. [incomplete]
1359	Bailiwick of Pagham	1496–7	2 pp. [summary]
1360	Bailiwicks of Aldington and Wingham, and 2 receipts	1497–8	3 mm. 2 atts.
1361	Bailiwick of Croydon	1501–2	3 pp. [incomplete]
2008	? Part of 1361: accounts for Hayes and Tring	c. 1500	3 pp.
2014	Bailiwick of South Malling	[1502–3]	5 pp. [incomplete]
1362	Bailiwicks of Croydon, Maidstone and Otford	[1508–9]	6 pp.
1363	Bailiwicks of Croydon and Pagham	1516–17	3 pp.
1364	Bailiwicks of Maidstone and Otford	[1518–19]	2 pp. [incomplete]
1365	Otford receipt	1519 January	1 p.
1366	Bailiwicks of Croydon, Maidstone and Otford	1522–3	6 pp.
1366A	Receipt: Croydon, Maidstone and Otford	1525–6	2 pp.
1367	Bailiwick of Otford	1533–4	3 pp.
1299	Bailiwick of Pagham [also accounts of various ministers]	1533–4	6 mm.
1368	Bailiwicks of Croydon and Otford	1536–7	3 mm.
1369	Bailiwick of Croydon	1541–2	2 mm.

1370	Bailiwicks of Aldington [parts] and Wingham, and lands exchanged with the King [Chislet, Northbourne and West Langdon]	1543–4	7 mm.
1371	Ibid.	1544–5	6 mm.
1372	Lands exchanged [including Malling (Kent), Great Cornard (Suffolk), Leybourne (Kent), Selhurst (Surrey), Arthington and Kirkstall (Yorks.), Heale (Devon), Leacon in Westwell (Kent) and Stoke St Milborough (Salop)]	1544–5	4 mm.
1373	Bailiwicks of Aldington and Wingham, and lands exchanged similar to 1370	1546–7	6 mm.
1374	Bailiwicks of Boughton and Croydon, and lands exchanged similar to 1372	1546–7	4 mm.
1375	Bailiwicks of Boughton, Croydon, Ringmer and Wingham	1548–9	7 mm.
1885	Bailiwicks of Boughton, Croydon, Ringmer [South Malling], and lands exchanged [cf. 1372]	1550–1	23 mm.
1376	Bailiwicks of Boughton, Croydon, Ringmer, West Langdon and Wingham	1552–3	8 mm.
1377	Ibid.	1554–5	7 mm.

(8) *Ministers' Accounts: general*

nos. 1378–1400,
1884, 1886–7, 2054–5

2054	Accounts of various ministers for Alkham rectory and lordship, bailiwick of Bilsington Priory, Blackwose manor in Saltwood, Brabourne rectory, Canterbury, St Gregory's bailiwick and Priory of St Sepulchre, Combe manor in Newington, Dover manor, Enbrook lordship, Hawkinge manor, Horton manor, West Langdon Priory, Linton manor, Paddlesworth manor in Lyminge, Pising manor in East Langdon, Postling in Hythe rectory, River manor, Satmar lordship and Sibertswold manor [all in Kent], Portslade rectory [Sussex], and rent from Purley in Croydon [Surrey]	1541–2	9 mm.
2055	Ibid.	1542–3	10 mm.
1378	Accounts of various ministers for Alkham rectory, Ashley in Northbourne rectory, Beauxfield rectory, Bekesbourne, Bilsington late Priory, Boughton, Brabourne rectory, Bredgar rectory, Buckholt, Canterbury, St Gregory's bailiwick and Westgate, Challock rectory, Chislet, Coldred manor, Combe manor in Newington, Craphill barn tithes with a pension from Hawkhurst rec-		

(1378 cont.) tory, Curlswood Park and Woolwich Wood in Nonington and Womenswold, Deal Prebend, Dover manor, Folkestone rectory, Ford and Herne rectory, Graveney rectory, Hawkinge manor, Hernhill rectory, Hull manor with Sholden rectory, Kennington rectory, rectories belonging to Langdon Priory, West Langdon rectory, Leacon in Westwell, Leeds rectory, Leysdown rectory, Littlebourne, Lydd rectory, Lydden rectory, Maidstone rectory, Marden rectory, Newland Grange in St Lawrence, Northbourne rectory, Pising manor in East Langdon, Postling in Hythe rectory, Reculver, River manor, St Nicholas at Wade rectory, Salmstone in St John the Baptist rectory, Satmar lordship, Selling rectory, Shelvingford, Sibertswold manor, Sittingbourne rectory, Stourmouth, portion of tithes in East Sutton, Tilmanstone rectory, Tonge rectory, Warehorn manor in St Nicholas at Wade, Westwell rectory, Whitstable rectory, Wingham College and Wye rectory [all in Kent], Brickhill rectory [Bucks.], Blackburn, Rochdale and Whalley rectories [Lancs.], Portslade rectory [Sussex], Croydon, Lambeth, Lambeth Wick, Levehurst in Lambeth, Purley Mead in Croydon, Selhurst, and Waddon in Croydon [all in Surrey]

	(1378 cont.) [all in Surrey]	1560–1	32 mm.
1379	Ibid.	1561–2	31 mm.
1380	Same as above, but omitting West Langdon rectory, and including Hastingleigh	1562–4	33 mm.
1381	Same as above, with account of the bailiff of the liberty of Croydon	1564–5	29 mm.
1382	Ibid.	1565–6	28 mm.
1383	,,	1567–8	28 mm.
1384	Vouchers relating mainly to the places mentioned above	1567	87 items
1385	Same as 1381	1568–9	27 mm.
1386	Same as above [arranged by county]	1571–2	27 mm.
1387	Ibid.	1572–3	22 mm.
1388	,,	1573–4	22 mm.
1389	Same as above. Also account of the tenths in the diocese of Canterbury, and account of the seneschal of the liberty in the county of Surrey	1576–7	24 mm.
1390	Ibid.	1577–8	24 mm.
1391	Same as above, but no account of the seneschal of the liberty of the county of Surrey, and also including Waldershare	1580–1	22 mm. 1 att.

392	Ibid.	1585–6	25 mm.
393	Same as above, but also including Longbeech in Westwell	1590–1	18 mm.
394	Ibid.	1591–2	20 mm.
395	,,	1592–3	19 mm.
396	,,	1593–4	19 mm.
397	,,	1594–5	23 mm.
398	,,	1596–7	18 mm.
399	,,	1597–8	20 mm.
400	Same as above, but also including Shulford Mead in Westgate [Canterbury], Southlands in Waldershare, and Walmer and Oxney rectories	1607–8	13 mm.
884	Same as above, but also including North Bishopsden Wood	1623–4	14 mm.
886	Accounts of the collector of corn and malt and "provider of muttons and hay": Boughton, Canterbury, St Gregory's, Chislet, Dover Priory possessions, Leysdown, Littlebourne, Newland Grange in St Lawrence, Reculver, Shelvingford and Westwell	1643	7 pp. 1 m.
887	Same as 1884, but also including an account of the tithes in Betteshanger, and Finglesham in Northbourne, and certain crop and wood accounts, and omitting the Lancashire manors	1644–5	20 mm.

(9) Receivers' Accounts: general

nos. 1401–26,
1888–91, 2028–35

1401   Account of receipts for Alkham rectory, Ash rectory, Ashley in Northbourne rectory, Beauxfield rectory, Bekesbourne, Bilsington, Boughton, Brabourne rectory, Bredgar rectory, Buckholt, Canterbury, St Gregory's and Westgate, Challock rectory, Chislet, Coldred manor, Combe in Newington, Craphill barn tithes in Wye, Curlswood Park and Woolwich Wood in Nonington and Womenswold, Deal Prebend, Dover manor, Folkestone rectory, Ford and Herne rectory, Graveney rectory, Hawkinge manor, Hernhill rectory, Hull manor with Sholden rectory, Kennington rectory, Leacon in Westwell, Leeds rectory, Leysdown rectory, Littlebourne, Lydd rectory, Lydden, Maidstone rectory, Maisendewe brooks, Marden rectory, Newland Grange in St Lawrence, Noning-

(1401 cont.)	ton rectory, Northbourne rectory, Overland in Ash rectory, Pising manor in East Langdon, Postling in Hythe rectory, Reculver, River manor, St Nicholas at Wade rectory, Salmstone in St John the Baptist rectory, Satmar, Selling rectory, Shelvingford, Sibertswold, Sittingbourne rectory, East Sutton tithes, Tilmanstone rectory, Tonge rectory, Walmer and Oxney rectories, Warehorn manor in St Nicholas at Wade, Westwell rectory and Wye rectory [all in Kent], Brickhill rectory [Bucks.], Blackburn, Rochdale and Whalley rectories [Lancs.], Portslade rectory [Sussex], and Croydon, Lambeth, Lambeth Wick, Levehurst in Lambeth, Purley Mead in Croydon, Selhurst, and Waddon in Croydon [all in Surrey], and rents of Christ Church, Canterbury, followed by payments for curates' stipends, repairs, officers' fees and pensions	1560–1	7 mm.
1402	Same as above, but no Christ Church rents	1561–2	8 mm
1403	Same as 1402. Also account of receipt for Hastingleigh	1562–4	8 mm.
1404	Same as 1401. Also account of receipts for Hastingleigh, and the tithes of Hoath	1564–5	8 mm.
1405	Same as above, also including a pension from Hawkhurst	1565–6	8 mm.
1406	Same as above, but no Hawkhurst entry, and also including accounts of tithes of the diocese, and of the seneschal of the liberty of the Archbishop	1567–8	8 mm.
1407	Ibid.	1568–9	11 mm.
1408	Same as above, but also including an entry for Ford Park	1571–2	9 mm.
1409	Same as 1407, but also including an account of the bailiff of the liberty of Croydon	1572–3	7 mm.
1410	Ibid.	1573–4	5 mm.
1411	,,	1575–6	6 mm.
1412	,,	1576–7	7 mm.
1413	,,	1577–8	7 mm.
1414	,,	1578–9	6 mm.
1415	Same as above, but also including an account for Waldershare rectory	1580–1	6 mm.
1416	Same as above, but omitting the account of the seneschal of the liberty	1583 July–Mich.	5 mm.
1417	Same as above	1585–6	5 mm.
1418	Ibid.	1586–7	5 mm.
1419	,,	1587–8	5 mm.
1420	,,	1588–9	5 mm.
1421	,,	1589–90	5 mm.

422	Same as above, but also including an account for Longbeech in Westwell	1590–1	5 mm.
423	Ibid.	1591–2	5 mm.
424	,,	1593–4	6 mm.
425	,,	1594–5	6 mm.
426	,,	1596–7	5 mm.
888	Schedule of arrears	1662	2 mm.
889	Account of receipts for Alkham, Ashley and Beauxfield rectories, Bekesbourne, Bilsington, Boughton, Brabourne rectory, Buckholt, Canterbury, St Gregory's and Westgate, Chislet, Coldred manor, Combe in Newington, Curlswood Park and Woolwich Wood in Nonington and Womenswold, Deal Prebend, Dover manor, Hawkinge with tithes in Evering and Swingfield, Hull and Sholden rectory, Leacon in Westwell, Leysdown rectory, Longbeech Wood, Lydden, Maidstone, Maisendewe brooks, Newland Grange in St Lawrence, Northbourne rectory, Pising manor in East Langdon, Postling in Hythe rectory, Reculver, River manor, St Nicholas at Wade rectory, Satmar manor, Shelvingford, Shulford Mead with land in Hastingleigh, Sibertswold, Stourmouth rectory, Tonge rectory, Waldershare rectory, Walmer rectory and Oxney tithes, Warehorn rectory, the rectories received from the exchange with Queen Elizabeth [Folkestone, Hernhill, Leeds, Challock, Bredgar, Selling, Graveney, Sittingbourne, Lydd, Kennington, Wye, Craphill barn tithes, Hawkhurst pension, Whitstable, Tilmanstone, Salmstone and East Sutton], and Wingham College rents [all in Kent], Brickhill rectory [Bucks.], Rochdale and Whalley rectories [Lancs.], Portslade rectory [Sussex], Croydon, Lambeth, Selhurst and Waddon [all in Surrey], and tithes in the diocese of Canterbury, followed by pensions and payments	1665–6	9 mm.
1890	Ibid.	1674–5	9 mm.
1891	,,	1677–8	9 mm.
2028	Day Book	1710–15	266 pp. [book]
2029	Accounts for same places as above	1765–81	105 ff. [book]
2030	,, ,, ,, ,, ,, ,,	1780–93	95 ff. [book]
2031	,, ,, ,, ,, ,, ,,	1805–16	48 ff. [book]
2031A	Wood accounts	1816	18 ff. [book]
2032	Accounts for Acol, Addington [Surrey], Alkham, Appledore, Ash, Buckland, Capel le		

(2032 *cont.*)	Ferne, Charlton, Chislet, Coldred, Doddington, Dover, Guston, Herne, Hernhill, Hoath, Hougham, Lynsted, Marden, Minster, Monkton, Northbourne, Reculver, St Nicholas at Wade, Stourmouth and Tonge	1874–5	12 ff. [book]
2033	Ibid.	1875–6	18 ff. [book]
2034	,,	1877	13 ff. [book]
2035	,,	1878	14 ff. [book]

(10) *Liberty of the Archbishop*

nos. 95–105, 1892–3

95	Steward	1418–19	6 mm.
96	,, [including Court of Otford fines]	1426–7	5 mm.
97	,,	1478–9	2 mm.
98	,,	1488–9	2 mm.
99	,,	1490–1	1 m.
100	Estreats of fines in King's Bench, Common Pleas, the Exchequer and Quarter Sessions, and issues of lands forfeited	1553	10 mm.
102	Estreats of fines	1558 Mich.	10 mm.
101	,, ,, ,,	1559–60	7 mm.
103	,, ,, ,,	*temp.* Philip and Mary [missing Aug. 1963]	1 m.
104	,, ,, ,,	*temp.* Philip and Mary	1 m.
105	Steward	1587–8	1 m.
104A	Estreats of fines	1679–80	3 mm.
1892	,, ,, ,,	1681–2	7 mm.
1893	,, ,, ,,	1682–3	5 mm.

II
CHRIST CHURCH CANTERBURY ESTATES: PRIOR AND CONVENT

A. COURT ROLLS
(1) *Individual properties in Kent*

DISHAM   no. 135
35   Courts and views   1438–9   1 m.

ANTERBURY, CALDICOTE IN   no. 290
90   Courts and views   1369   1 m.
      [The manor was given by Archbishop Rey-
      nolds to Christ Church in 1326: see R. A. L.
      Smith, *Canterbury Cathedral Priory*, Cam-
      bridge, 1943, 46]

LIFFE, WEST [NEAR ROCHESTER]   no. 1101
101   Courts and views   1434–5   1 m.

YDDEN   MS. 95[38]
1S. 95[38]   Last of the marsh   1424 April 10   1 p.

YMPNE, COURT-AT-STREET IN   no. 973
73   Courts and views [Boroughs of Street and
      Minster]   1510–40   58 pp.
      [Property of the sacrist: see R. A. L.
      Smith, *Canterbury Cathedral Priory*, 24
      and 92]

ONKTON   nos. 721–2A
21   Court [View at Brooks End]   1395 Oct.–Nov.   1 m.
22   Extracts of courts   1397–1422   1 p.
22A   Extracts and a rental [also Dane Court in St
      Peter's Thanet]   1397–1444   4 pp. [book]

(2) *Grouped properties in Kent*

                                          MS. 951/1[33]
1S. 951/1[33]   Courts and views at Appledore,
      Great Chart, West Cliffe, Fairfield, Fil-
      borough in Chalk, Godmersham, Mer-
      sham, Orpington, Ruckinge and West-   1536 May–   12 mm.
      well   1539 Oct.

45

(3) *The Prior and Obedientiaries*

ALTA CURIA OF THE PRIOR nos. 1–20

1	Court	1329–30	1 m.
2	Courts	(b) 1359–60	8 mm.
		(a) 1365	
3	„ [including a will in French]	1361	3 mm.
4	„	1365	1 m.
5	„	1369–70	9 mm.
6	„	1371–2	6 mm
7	„	1372–3	9 mm.
8	„	1400–1	10 mm.
9	„	1402–3	9 mm. 1 p.
10	„	1404–5	9 mm.
11	„	1408–9	6 mm
12	„ [Views at Seasalter]	1410	1 m.
13	„	1410–11	2 mm.
14	„	1411–12	4 mm.
15	„	1412–13, 1413–14	2 mm.
16	„	1413–15	5 mm.
17	„	1415–16	6 mm.
18	Amercements	1439–40	1 m.
19	„	1440–1	1 m.
20	Estreats	1440–1	1 m.

CAMPANILE COURT OF THE SACRISTAN no. 28

28	Views and courts	1510–40	60 pp.

B. ACCOUNT ROLLS

(1) *Individual properties by counties:* *Devon, Essex, Kent and London*

Devon

DOCCOMBE no. 2056

2056	Rental	1472	2 pp.
	[with copy of a rental of 1289, and of a charter of Henry de la Pomeroy, late 12th cent.]		

Essex

LALLING no. 544

544	Reeve	1326–7	2 mm.
	[see Morant's *Hist. of Essex* i, 354–5]		

Kent

ACOL no. 133

133	Rental of new rents	c. 1286	1 m.

ADISHAM		nos. 133A, 134	
133A	Rental of obits for lands [also at Monkton]	*temp.* Edward I	3 mm.
134	Serjeant	1368–9	2 mm.

APPLEDORE		nos. 191–211		
191	Serjeant	1330–1		3 mm.
192	,,	1338–9		1 m.
193	,,	1346–7		2 mm.
194	,,	1385–6		3 mm.
195	Bedell and rent collector	1393–4		1 m.
196	,, ,, ,, ,,	1395–6		1 m.
197	Farmers	1398–9		2 mm.
198	Farmer and surveyor of the wall and grange	1416–17		2 mm.
199	,, ,, ,, ,, ,, ,, ,, ,,	1418–19		2 mm.
200	Surveyor of the wall and grange	1423		1 m.
201	Farmer [and repair sheet]	1429–30		2 mm.
202	Surveyor, farmer and bedell	1435–7		2 mm.
203	Farmer and surveyor of the wall and repairs	1441	13 pp.	[book]
204	Bedell and rent collector, and farmer	1453–4		1 m.
205	,, ,, ,, ,, ,, ,,	1458–9		1 m.
206	Bedell and rent collector, and surveyor of the wall	1464–5	1 m.	1 p.
207	Bedell and rent collector	1465–6		1 m.
208	Surveyor of the wall	1465–6		1 m.
209	Bedell and rent collector	1468–9		1 m.
210	,, ,, ,, ,,	1471–2		1 m.
211	,, ,, ,, ,,	1476–7		1 m.

CANTERBURY, CALDICOTE IN		no. 2047	
2047	Rental	1508–9	1 m.

CHART, GREAT		nos. 304–8, 1464	
305	Serjeant	1305–6	2 mm.
304	,,	1325–6 [or 1292–3]	3 mm.
306	,,	1335–6	2 mm.
307	Rental	[*temp.* Henry VII]	1 p.
308	Farmer's inventory	[*temp.* Henry VI–VII]	1 p.
1464	Title to a rent due to the manor	1527	2 pp.

CLIFFE, WEST, RECTORY [NEAR DOVER]		no. 1100	
1100	Farmer [also vouchers]	1421–3	3 mm. 1 p.

EASTRY		nos. 379–434	
379	Serjeant	1319–20	2 mm.
380	,,	1322–3	3 mm. 1 att.
381	,,	1323–4	3 mm. 1 att.
382	,,	1325–6	4 mm.
383	,,	1325–6	2 mm.
384	,,	1326–7	3 mm.

47

385	Serjeant	1376-7	2 mm
386	Serjeant, bedell and rent collector	1382-3	3 mm
387	Serjeant	1384-5	2 pp.
388	Bedell and rent collector	1385-6	1 m.
389	,, ,, ,, ,,	1387-9	1 m.
390	Bedell, rent collector and farmer	1392-3	1 m.
391	Bedell and rent collector	1395-6	1 m.
392	,, ,, ,, ,,	1396-7	1 m.
393	,, ,, ,, ,,	1411-12	1 m.
394	,, ,, ,, ,,	1413-22	6 mm.
395	,, ,, ,, ,,	1416-17	1 m.
397	Inventory	1418 Mich.	1 m.
398	Bedell and rent collector	1420-1	1 m.
399	,, ,, ,, ,,	1423-4	2 mm
402	,, ,, ,, ,,	1427-8	2 mm.
403	,, ,, ,, ,,	1429-30	1 m.
405	,, ,, ,, ,,	1430-1	1 m.
406	,, ,, ,, ,,	1431-2	1 m.
407	,, ,, ,, ,,	1432-3	1 m.
408	,, ,, ,, ,,	1433-4	1 m.
409	,, ,, ,, ,,	1435-6	1 m.
410	,, ,, ,, ,,	1437-8	1 m.
411	,, ,, ,, ,,	1438-9	1 m.
412	,, ,, ,, ,,	1440-1	1 m.
413	,, ,, ,, ,,	1445-6	1 m.
414	,, ,, ,, ,,	1446-7	1 m.
415	,, ,, ,, ,,	1448-9	1 m.
416	,, ,, ,, ,,	1449-50	1 m.
418	,, ,, ,, ,,	1453-4	1 m.
419	,, ,, ,, ,,	1454-5	1 m.
420	,, ,, ,, ,,	1457-8	1 m.
421	,, ,, ,, ,,	1461-2	1 m.
423	,, ,, ,, ,,	1463-4	1 m.
424	,, ,, ,, ,,	1464-5	1 m.
425	,, ,, ,, ,,	1465-6	1 m.
426	,, ,, ,, ,,	1466-7	1 m.
427	,, ,, ,, ,,	1467-8	1 m.
428	,, ,, ,, ,,	1469-70	1 m.
429	,, ,, ,, ,,	1471-2	1 m.
431	,, ,, ,, ,,	1472-3	1 m.
432	,, ,, ,, ,,	1474-5	1 m.
433	,, ,, ,, ,,	1476-7	1 m.
434	Collector	1521-2	3 mm.

EASTRY RECTORY

396	Serjeant	1417-18	1 m.
400	,, [manor also]	1426-7	1 m.
401	,,	1427-8	1 m.
404	,,	1429-30	1 p.
417	,, [manor also]	1450-1	1 p.
417A	,,	1451-2	2 pp.

422	Serjeant	1462–3	2 pp.
430	,,	1471–2	2 pp.
ELHAM		no. 435	
435	Rentals	early 15th cent.	13 items
FAIRFIELD RECTORY		no. 443	
443	Farmer	1420–1	1 m.
FARLEIGH, EAST		no. 447	
447	Bedell and rent collector	1458–9	1 m.
HALSTOW, LOWER, BARKSORE IN		no. 230	
230	Serjeant	1304–5	2 mm.
HOLLINGBOURNE		nos. 495–524, 2048, MSS. 791, 793, 794, 1025[6]	
495	Serjeant, bedell and rent collector	1372–3	4 mm.
496	Farmer [Loose also]	1376–89	1 p.
497	Bedell and rent collector	1418–19	1 m.
498	,, ,, ,, ,,	1422–8	11 mm.
499	,, ,, ,, ,,	1428–9	2 mm.
500	,, ,, ,, ,,	1429–30	2 mm.
501	,, ,, ,, ,,	1430–1	2 mm.
502	,, ,, ,, ,,	1431–2	1 m. 1 att.
503	,, ,, ,, ,,	1439–40	1 m.
504	,, ,, ,, ,,	1443–4	1 m.
505	,, ,, ,, ,,	1446–7	1 m.
506	,, ,, ,, ,,	1447–8	1 m.
507	,, ,, ,, ,,	1448–9	1 m.
508	,, ,, ,, ,,	1451–2	1 m.
509	,, ,, ,, ,,	1452–3	1 m.
510	,, ,, ,, ,,	1453–4	1 m.
511	,, ,, ,, ,,	1458–9	1 m.
512	,, ,, ,, ,,	1460–1	1 m.
513	,, ,, ,, ,,	1463–4	1 m.
514	,, ,, ,, ,,	1464–5	1 m.
515	,, ,, ,, ,,	1466–7	1 m.
516	,, ,, ,, ,,	1467–8	1 m.
MS. 794	Rental	[1467–8]	67 ff. [book]
517	Bedell and rent collector	1468–9	1 m.
518	,, ,, ,, ,,	1469–70	1 m.
519	,, ,, ,, ,,	1470–1	1 m.
520	,, ,, ,, ,,	1471–2	1 m.
521	,, ,, ,, ,,	1472–3	1 m.
522	,, ,, ,, ,,	1475–6	1 m.
523	,, ,, ,, ,,	1476–7	1 m.
MS. 1025[6]	Rental	1493	9 ff. [book]
MS. 793	Rental	1497–8	13 ff. [book]
524	Rental	1504 Mich.	1 p.

E

2048	Rental	late 15th or	
		early 16th cent.	18 pp.
MS. 791	Rental	1516–17	9 ff. [book]

ICKHAM   nos. 534–9, 1449,
                                                         2049, MSS. 952[54],
                                                         1025[7], 1094[12]

534	Rental	c. 1480	5 mm
535	,,	1427–8	1 p.
536	Bedell	1437–8	1 p.
537	Keeper	1446–7	1 m.
538	Indenture for delivery of stock to the farmer	1458	2 pp.
MS. 1094[12]	Rental	15th cent.	22 ff. [book]
1449	Rental of places including Ickham Dean [? Christ Church, Canterbury]	late 15th cent.	2 pp. [incomplete]
MS. 952[54]	Rental	late 15th cent.	6 ff. [incomplete]
2049	Rental	late 15th cent.	1 p.
539	,,	1515	2 pp.
MS. 1025[7]	Survey and custumal	c. 1500–20	12 ff. [book]

MERSHAM   no. 720

| 720 | Rental and custumal | late 14th cent. | 4 mm. |

MONGEHAM   MS. 790

| MS. 790 | Rental and survey | 1395–6 | 1 m. |

MONKTON   nos. 133A, 723–53,
                                                         MS. 798

133A	Rental of obits for lands [also at Adisham]	temp. Edward I	3 mm.
723	Bedell and rent collector	1387–8	1 m.
724	,, ,, ,, ,,	1422–3, 1424–5, 1425–6, 1426–7	6 mm.
725	,, ,, ,, ,,	1428–9	2 mm.
726	,, ,, ,, ,,	1431–2	1 m.
727	,, ,, ,, ,,	1435–6	1 m.
728	,, ,, ,, ,,	1439–40	1 m.
729	,, ,, ,, ,,	1440–1	1 m.
730	,, ,, ,, ,,	1441–2	1 m.
731	,, ,, ,, ,,	1442–3	1 m.
732	,, ,, ,, ,,	1444–5	1 m.
733	,, ,, ,, ,,	1446–7	1 m.
734	,, ,, ,, ,,	1448–9	1 m.
735	Farmer	1451–2	1 p.
736	Bedell and rent collector	1454–5	1 m.
737	Serjeant [with Birchington Grange]	1455–6	2 pp.
738	Serjeant of the rectory [with Birchington Grange]	1456–7	2 pp.
739	Bedell and rent collector	1457–8	1 m.
740	,, ,, ,, ,,	1458–9	1 m.

˝41	Serjeant of the rectory [with Birchington Grange]	1460–1	2 pp.
˝42	Bedell and rent collector	1462–3	1 m.
˝43	,, ,, ,, ,,	1463–4	1 m.
˝44	,, ,, ,, ,,	1464–5	1 m.
˝45	Serjeant of the rectory [with Birchington Grange]	1464–5	2 pp.
˝46	Bedell and rent collector	1469–70	1 m.
˝47	,, ,, ,, ,,	1470–1	1 m.
˝48	Serjeant of the rectory [with Birchington Grange]	1470–1	3 pp.
˝49	Bedell and rent collector	1471–2	1 m.
˝50	Serjeant of the rectory [with Birchington Grange]	1471–2	2 pp.
˝51	Bedell and rent collector	1472–3	1 m.
˝52	Serjeant [with Birchington Grange]	1472–3	2 pp.
753	Bedell and rent collector	1474–5	1 m.
MS. 798	Rental	1494–1500	30 ff. [book]

NEWCHURCH, GOOGY HALL IN   nos. 467–72

467	Farmers [lands in Ivychurch and Hope All Saints also, parcels of the manor of Googy Hall]	1427–8	3 mm.
468	Farmer	1430–1	1 m.
469	,,	1477–8	1 p.
470	,,	1483–4	1 p.
471	,,	1485–6	1 p.
472	,,	1486–7	1 p.
	[The Prior of Christ Church, Canterbury, acted as farmer of the manor for All Souls' College, Oxford]		

THANET   no. 1072

1072	Collectors [? Christ Church, Canterbury]	c. 1500	1 m.

WESTWELL   nos. 1106–10, 2057

1106	Rental	c. 1280–1300	10 mm.
1106A	Serjeant	1365–6	3 mm.
1107	Serjeant, bedell and rent collector	1367–8	3 mm.
1108	,, ,, ,, ,, ,,	1369–70	3 mm.
1109	,, ,, ,, ,, ,, [including indenture as to delivery of stock]	1372–3	3 mm. 1 att.
1110	Serjeant	1385–6	2 mm.
2057	Terrier of lands belonging to the manor	1528–9	2 mm.

WESTWELL, LONGBEECH WOOD IN   no. 591

591	Forester	1342–3	1 m.

London

nos. 608, 2013

2013	Rent collector and rentals	*c.* 1500	4 pp. [fragments]
608	Rent collector	1510–11	2 mm.

(2) *Grouped properties for Essex and Kent*

MS. 951/1[34]

MS. 951/1[34]   Bedell and rent collector for Lalling [Essex], West Cliffe and Meopham [also chamberlain's account]   1525–6   7 mm. [incomplete]

(3) *General*

MS. 833

MS. 833   Receipts and payments   1467 Mich.–1468 Nov.   77 ff. [book]

(4) *The Prior and Obedientiaries*

ALMONER   nos. 29–36

29	Accounts of Peter de Sales	1361–2	2 mm.
30	,, ,, ,, ,, ,,	1363–4	2 mm.
31	,, ,, ,, ,, ,,	1364–5	2 mm.
32	View or summary of the state of the office	1431–2	1 m.
33	,, ,, ,, ,, ,, ,, ,, ,, ,,	1432–3	1 m.
34	,, ,, ,, ,, ,, ,, ,, ,, ,,	1439–40	1 m.
35	,, ,, ,, ,, ,, ,, ,, ,, ,,	1472–3	3 pp.
36	,, ,, ,, ,, ,, ,, ,, ,, ,,	[*temp.* Henry VI]	1 m.

ANNIVERSARIAN   nos. 37–52, MS. 789

37   Accounts [provision of fish for Lent, vigil of Christmas etc. for the convent]   1341–2   3 mm.
MS. 789   Rental [Adisham, Challock, Little Chart, Godmersham, Langdon, Osterland (unid.) and Peckham]   1374–1477   76 ff. [book: draft]

37A	Accounts	1429–30	1 m.
38	,,	1430–1	1 m.
39	,,	1438–9	1 m.
40	,,	1442–3	1 m.
41	,,	1465–6	1 m.
42	,,	[1467–8]	1 m.
43	,,	1474–5	1 m.
44	,,	1475–6	1 m.
45	,,	1496–7	1 m.
46	,,	1500–1	1 m.
47	,,	1504–5	1 m.

48	Accounts		1516–17	1 m.
49	,,		1521–2	1 m.
50	,,		1522–3	1 m.
51	,,		1528–9	1 m.
52	,,		1535–6	1 m.

BARTONER

nos. 53–7

53	Accounts [Malthalle]		1438–41	2 mm.
54	,,	,,	1450–1	1 m.
55	,,	,,	1466–7	1 m.
56	,,	,,	1468–9	1 m.
57	,,	,,	1471–2	1 m.

CELLARER

nos. 58–67, 2009

58	Accounts	1430–1	2 mm.
59	,,	1438–9	1 m.
60	,,	1444–5	1 m.
2009	,,	1446–7	1 m. [heading lacking]
61	,,	1447–8	1 m.
62	,,	1449–50	1 m.
63	,,	1450–1	2 mm.
64	,,	1458–9	1 m.
65	,,	1466–7	1 m.
66	,,	1480–1	1 m.
67	,,	1517–18	9 pp.

HORDARIAN

nos. 68–9

68	Accounts	1311–12	2 mm.
69	,,	1391–2	1 m.

INFIRMARER

no. 70

70	Account	1402–3	1 m.

MONK WARDENS

nos. 71–3

71	Accounts	1427–8	2 mm.
71A	,,	1430–1	1 m.
71B	,,	1432–3	1 m.
72	,,	1436–7	7 mm.
73	,,	1437–8	7 mm.

PRIOR

no. 74

74	Account, rentals, oblations, obventions, expenses, stipends, "new work" [m.5]	1446–7	5 mm.

SACRISTAN

nos. 75–9, 1442, 1458, 2059–61

75	Accounts	1430–1	1 m.
76	,,	1433–4	1 m.
1442	Rental, and inquisition about rents taken at Godmersham	1454	1 m. 1 p.

77	Accounts	1461–2	1 m.
78	,,	1475–6	1 m.
*79	,,	1476–7	1 m.
2059	Rental	15th cent.	2 mm.
1458	Articles and questions to be asked about 12 acres of land let to farm by the Sacrist in Romney Marsh	1521 May	2 pp.
2060	Rental	1533	2 mm. [book]
2061	,,	1534	2 mm. [book]

*[see C. E. Woodruff, "The Sacrist's Rolls of Christ Church, Canterbury" in *Archaeologia Cantiana* xlviii (1936), 38–80]

TREASURERS

nos. 80–91,
MSS. 951/1[31],
[32], 1025[8]

MS. 1025[8]	Accounts	1356–7	6 mm. [summarised book form]
80	Accounts	1406–7	4 mm.
81	,,	1419–20	4 mm.
82	,,	1449–50	4 mm.
83	,,	1456–7	4 mm.
84	,,	1459–60	3 mm.
84A	,,	c. 1461–83	8 pp. [draft]
85	,,	c. 1461–83	6 pp. [draft]
86	,,	1500–1	6 mm. [handsome initials with mottos]
87	,,	c. 1500	1 m. [incomplete]
88	,,	1508–9	7 mm.
MS. 951/1[31]	Accounts	1509–10	8 mm. [book]
MS. 951/1[32]	,,	1512–13	8 mm. [book]
89	Accounts	1517–18	8 mm.
90	,,	1518–19	8 mm.
91	,, [vouchers for pittances]	1525–6	2 pp.

(5) *Liberty of the Prior of Christ Church*

nos. 106–18A

106	Accounts of the Stewards and Bailiffs [chiefly estreats of fines in King's Bench, Common Pleas, the Exchequer and Quarter Sessions]	1323–4	4 mm.
107	Ibid.	1431–2	1 m.
107A	,,	1436–7	1 p.
108	,,	1439	1 m.
109	,,	1443–4	1 m.
110	,,	1482–3	1 p.
111	,,	1486–7	1 m.
112	,,	1491–2	1 p.
113	,,	1499–1500	1 p. 1 att.

114	Ibid.	1501–2	1 m.
115	Same as above [Kent]	1502–3	1 m.
116	Ibid.	1504–5	1 p.
117	,,	1508–9	1 m.
118A	,,	1509–10	1 p.
118	,,	1510–11	1 m.

CHRIST CHURCH CANTERBURY ESTATES: DEAN AND CHAPTER

A. COURT ROLLS

(1) *Grouped properties for Kent*

nos. 1159–61

1159	Views at Adisham, Chart, Eastry, Ickham [court also], Monkton, and Seasalter [court also]	1547 October	1 m.
1160	Views and courts at Adisham, Appledore, Caldicote in Canterbury [view only], Great Chart, Copton in Preston [view only], Eastry, Fairfield, Godmersham, Hollingbourne, Ickham, Leysdown, Mersham, Monkton and Seasalter. Courts at Brook, Chartham, Meopham and Ruckinge	1586–7	10 ff. [book]
1161	Same as above, except no views and courts at Caldicote and Leysdown, no courts at Meopham, but views and courts also at Loose and Ruckinge	1593–4	12 ff. [book]

(2) *Alta Curia of the Dean and Chapter*

nos. 21–7

21	Courts	1561–3	2 mm.
22	,,	1571–2	2 mm.
23	,, [containing writs and jury lists as well as pleas]	1579–80	2 files
24	Courts	1581–2	6 mm.
25	,,	1584–5	8 mm.
26	,,	1620–2	3 mm.
27	,,	1625–6	2 mm.

B. ACCOUNT ROLLS

(1) *Individual properties by counties: Devon, Kent, Surrey and Sussex*

Devon

DOCCOMBE

no. 362

| 362 | Rental or survey of tenants | 1572 | 2 mm. |

55

Kent

ACOL			no. 754	
754	Rental [also of Monkton and Birchington] in English		1548	3 mm.

CANTERBURY			no. 2062, MSS. 796, 797, 814, 841[22], 942[10], 952[53]	
MS. 814	Rental [no arrears]		1564–5	24 ff. [book]
2062	Rental of quitrents		1582	24 ff. [book]
MS. 796	Rental [arrears]		1582–6	50 ff. [book]
MS. 841[22]	Rental [no arrears]. Also Chartham, Lower Hardres, Wadenhull manor in Waltham, and Wingham		1593–7	24 ff. [book]
MS. 952[53]	Rental [arrears]		1607–8	22 ff. [book]
MS. 942[10]	,, ,, . Also Lower Hardres		1618 Mich.	23 ff. [book]
MS. 797	Rental [arrears]		1618–19	30 ff. [book]

HOLLINGBOURNE			MSS. 791, 795	
MS. 795	Rental		1549–50	14 ff. [book]
MS. 791	Terrier of the demesne		1603	4 mm.

TENTERDEN PARSONAGE			nos. 1041–2, 2052	
1041	Rental		1562	1 m.
1042	Rental and terrier		1572	1 m.
2052	Terrier		1577	1 m.

WHITSTABLE, SEASALTER IN			no. 2053	
2053	Terrier of the manor and parsonage		1621	1 m.

Surrey

NEWINGTON, WALWORTH IN			no. 2050	
2050	Terrier of the demesne		1623	1 m.

Sussex

PAGHAM PARSONAGE			no. 2065	
2065	Glebe terrier		1576	1 m.

(2) *Treasurer of the Dean and Chapter*

			nos. 92–4	
92	Accounts [Dean's and prebendaries' portions, stipends of preachers, minor canons etc., expenses of the Church]		1547–8	19 pp. [p.14 fol. blank]
93	Ibid.		1555–6	10 pp.
94	,,		1597–8	8 pp.

(3) *Liberty of the Dean and Chapter*

nos. 119–32A

119	Accounts [chiefly estreats of fines in King's Bench, Common Pleas, the Exchequer and Quarter Sessions, and mainly relating to Kent]	1578–9	8 mm.
120	Ibid.	1579–80	8 mm.
121	,,	1580–1	8 mm.
131	,,	c. 1583	1 m.
122	,,	1584–5	11 mm.
123	,,	1585–6	3 mm.
124	,,	1587–9	2 mm.
126	,,	c. 1588	1 m.
125	,,	c. 1590	10 mm.
127	,,	1592–3	10 mm.
128	,,	1595	1 m.
130	,,	1595 July	1 m.
129	,,	1595–6	8 mm.
132	,,	c. 1600	1 m.
132A	,,	1636–7	1 m.

III
PRIOR AND CONVENT
OF ROCHESTER'S ESTATES

ACCOUNT ROLLS
of individual properties in Kent

HOO PARSONAGE   no. 525
525   Rental   *temp.* Henry VI   1 m.

SOUTHFLEET   no. 968
968   Bedell   1393–4   1 m.   1 att.
       [and see MS. 952(93) Courts and views
       1510–27   17 ff. (book)]

IV
ESTATES OF OTHER KENTISH
RELIGIOUS HOUSES

ACCOUNT ROLLS

CANTERBURY, ST AUGUSTINE'S ABBEY		nos. 298–9, 2058, 2071	
2058	Treasurer	1446–7	5 mm.
298	,,	1459–60	22 pp.
299	Valor of lands etc., totals only	1522–3	1 p.
2071	Rental of lands once belonging to, including Littlebourne and Bridge	c. 1540	2 pp.
FAVERSHAM ABBEY		nos. 449, 2006, 2070	
449	[Treasurer] details of income and payments	c. 1490	3 pp.
2006 } 2070 }	Valor	c. 1538–59	10 pp.
MINSTER IN SHEPPEY, PRIORY OF ST SEXBURGA		no. 954	
954	Valor	c. 1535	4 pp.
ST RADEGUND'S ABBEY [Blackwose, al. Canons Court, in Saltwood]*		no. 270	
270	Keeper's account and rental	1391–2	1 m. 1 p.

270 ... *[Premonstratensian house, cell of Lavendon, united c. 1377 (?) to the abbey of St Radegund, which with its properties was granted to Archbishop Cranmer in 1536, who shortly afterwards returned it to the Crown (*Mon.* vi. 940 and K. & H., 163)]

59

V
BATH AND WELLS ESTATES: BISHOP
A. COURT ROLLS
(1) *Individual properties in Somerset*

AXBRIDGE · · · · · · · no. 213

213 · Court of the tourn [hallmoot at Blackford] · 1379
March and April 1 m.

BANWELL · · · · · · · nos. 214–21

214 · Hallmoot [hallmoot at Compton Bishop, legal
hundred at Winterstoke] · 1362 · 2 mm.
215 · Hallmoot [hallmoot at Compton Bishop] · 1369 · 1 m.
216 · Hundred at Winterstoke · *temp.* Richard II · 1 m.
[incomplete]

217 · Hundreds of pleas [hundred of pleas at Congresbury and Yatton] · 1470–1 · 10 mm.
218 · Hallmoots · 1500 · 1 m.
219 · Court of the tourn and hundreds of pleas · *temp.* Henry VII · 2 mm.
220 · Hallmoots · 1560–1 · 1 m.
221 · ,, · 1559–65 · 14 pp. [draft]

CHARD · · · · · · · nos. 327–34

327 · Legal hundred and hallmoot · 1362 · 1 m.
328 · ,, ,, ,, ,, [hallmoot at
Buckland and legal hundred and hallmoot
at Wellington] · 1362 · 1 m.
329 · Legal hundred and hallmoot · 1379 · 1 m.
330 · Court of the tourn [burgus] · 1379 · 1 m.
331 · ,, ,, ,, ,, ,, [Court of the
tourn at Wellington burgus] · 1414 · 1 m.
332 · Legal hundred and hallmoot [legal hundred
at Winsham] · 1414 · 1 m.
333 · Legal hundred, hallmoot and court of the
tourn [legal hundred at Winsham] · 1444 · 1 m.
334 · Legal hundred and hallmoot [hallmoot at
Buckland, and hundred and hallmoot at
Wellington] · 1464 · 1 m.

CONGRESBURY · · · · · · · nos. 350–1

350 · Hallmoot [pleas at Wells, legal hundred at
Axbridge] · 1277 or 1312 · 2 mm.
351 · Legal hundred and hallmoot [Yatton] [hall-
moot at Yatton, legal hundred and hallmoot at Chew, and legal hundreds at
Hampton and Claverton] · 1379 · 5 mm.

60

EVERCREECH nos. 438–9

| 438 | Hallmoot [hallmoot at Cranmore] | 1379 | 1 m. |
| 439 | ,,   ,,   ,,   ,, | 1414 | 1 m. |

HUISH nos. 529–30

| 529 | Hundreds [hundreds at Bishop's Lydeard, Chard, Kingsbury, Wellington and Wiveliscombe] | 1438–9 | 7 mm. |
| 530 | Hundred and hallmoot [hundred and hallmoot at Kingsbury] | 1464 | 1 m. |

KINGSBURY EPISCOPI nos. 541–2

| 541 | Hundred and hallmoot | 1362 | 1 m. |
| 542 | Legal hundred and hallmoot | 1444 | 1 m. |

LYDEARD, BISHOP'S nos. 609–12

609	Legal hundred and hallmoot	1362 May	1 m.
610	,, ,, ,, ,,	1414 May	1 m.
611	Hallmoot	1500 May	1 m.
612	Hallmoots [hallmoots at Westbury and Compton Bishop]	1548–9	1 m.

WELLINGTON nos. 1094–6

1094	Legal hundred and hallmoot [hallmoot at Buckland]	1312 December [or 1277]	1 m.
1095	Legal hundred, hallmoot and court of the tourn [burgus] [hallmoot at Buckland]	1362 May	2 mm.
1096	Legal hundred and hallmoot [hallmoot at Buckland]	1414 May	1 m.

WELLS nos. 1097–9

1097	[Burgus] Legal hundred [legal hundred at Cheddar]	1312 November	1 m.
1098	[Forum] Legal hundred	1312 November	1 m.
1098A	[Manor] Hallmoot [hallmoots at Westbury and Wookey]	1464 June	1 m.
1099	[Burgus] Courts	1510–11	10 mm.

WINSHAM no. 1124

| 1124 | Courts of the tourn | 1542–3 Oct.–April | 1 m. |

WIVELISCOMBE nos. 1125–30

1125	Legal hundred, court of the tourn [burgus] and hallmoot	1379 April	2 mm.
1126	Legal hundred, court of the tourn [burgus] and hallmoot	1414 May	1 m.
1127	Hallmoot, hundred and view [also hallmoot at Buckland and view at Wellington (Burgus)]	1464 April	1 m.

1128	View [view, hundred and hallmoot at Bishop's Lydeard]	1464 April	1 m.
1129	Hallmoot	1500 May	1 m.
1130	,, [hallmoot at Bishop's Lydeard]	1549 April	1 m.

(2) *Grouped properties for Somerset and Gloucestershire*

nos. 1176–92

1176	Legal hundreds and hallmoots [courts] at Axbridge, Banwell and Winterstoke, Bishop's Lydeard, Blackford, Buckland, Chard [and burgus], Cheddar, Chew, Cranmore, Evercreech, Hampton and Claverton, Huish, Kingsbury, Wellington [and burgus], Wells [forum and manor], Westbury, Winsham, Wiveliscombe [and burgus], Wookey, Yatton and Congresbury [all in Somerset], and Pucklechurch [Glos.]	1342–3	24 mm.
1177	Same as above, but omitting Axbridge, Banwell and Winterstoke	1353 [Hockday and St John Baptist only]	19 mm.
1178	Same as 1176, but including Bath and Compton Bishop, and omitting Winterstoke	1361 [Hockday and St John Baptist only]	25 mm.
1179	Same as above, but omitting Banwell and Winterstoke, Bath, Compton Bishop, and Pucklechurch [Glos.]	1369 [Mich. only]	17 mm.
1180	Same as 1176, but including Compton Bishop, and omitting Axbridge, Bishop's Lydeard, Blackford, Chard, Wellington [burgus], Wells [forum], Winsham, Winterstoke, Wiveliscombe, and Pucklechurch [Glos.]	1373 July	10 mm.
1181	Same as 1176, but including Bath, and omitting Banwell and Winterstoke, Huish, Winsham, and Pucklechurch [Glos.]	1382 [Mich. only]	18 mm.
1182	Same as above, but also omitting Hampton and Claverton and Westbury	1383 Mich.	21 mm.
1183	Same as 1176, but omitting Axbridge, Banwell and Winterstoke, Huish, Winsham, and Pucklechurch [Glos.]	1384 July	9 mm.
1184	Same as 1176, but including Compton Bishop, and omitting Axbridge, Huish, Winsham, Winterstoke, and Pucklechurch [Glos.]	1390 July	14 mm.
1185	Same as 1176, but including Compton Bishop, and omitting Axbridge, Huish, Winsham, Wookey, and Pucklechurch [Glos.]	1395 Jan. [Candlemas]	12 mm.
1186	Same as 1176, but including Bath and Comp-		

(1186 cont.)	ton Bishop, and omitting Huish, and Pucklechurch [Glos.]	1421 April	18 mm.
1187	Same as 1176, but including Compton Bishop, and omitting Axbridge and Winsham	1424 July [St John Baptist]	13 mm.
1188	Same as 1176, but including Bath, and omitting Banwell and Winterstoke, Huish, and Pucklechurch [Glos.]	1432 May [Hockday]	19 mm.
1189	Same as 1176, but including Westerleigh and Wick [Glos.], and omitting Axbridge, Banwell and Winterstoke, Hampton, Winsham, and Yatton and Congresbury	1440 July [St John Baptist]	7 mm.
1190	Evercreech, Wellington, Wells and Wick only	1513–14 Mich. and Hockday	4 mm.
1191	Same as 1176, but including Compton Bishop, Westerleigh [Glos.], Wick [Glos.], and Worle, and omitting Axbridge, Blackford, Cranmore, Evercreech, Hampton and Claverton, Wells [forum], Winsham and Winterstoke	1539 Mich.	7 mm.
1192	Banwell, Huish, Wells and Westbury only	1595–6 Mich.–April	5 mm.

B. ACCOUNT ROLLS

(1) *Individual properties in Hampshire and Somerset*

Hampshire

DOGMERSFIELD		nos. 363–4	
363	Rent collector and bailiff	1426–7	3 mm.
364	,, ,, ,, ,,	1432–3	2 mm.

Somerset

BANWELL		nos. 222–4	
222	Reeve	1443–4	4 mm.
223	,,	1473–4	3 mm.
224	,,	1499–1500	2 mm.
BUCKLAND		nos. 286A–7	
286A	Reeve	1434–5	2 mm.
287	,,	1443	1 m.
CHEDDAR		nos. 324–5	
324	Reeve	1446–7	3 mm.
325	,,	1494–5	3 mm.
COMPTON BISHOP		nos. 347–9	
347	Reeve	1422–3	2 mm.
348	,,	1442–3	1 m.

349   Reeve   1451–2   1 m.

CRANMORE   no. 354
354   Reeve   1401–2   2 mm.

EVERCREECH   nos. 440–2
440   Reeve   1382–3   4 mm.
441   ,,   1418–19   3 mm.
442   ,,   1431–2   3 mm.

WIVELISCOMBE   nos. 1131–2
1131   Reeve   1443–4   3 mm.
1132   ,,   1463–4   3 mm.

WOOKEY   no. 1133
1133   Reeve   1461–2   3 mm.

YATTON   no. 1158
1158   Reeve [profits divided between the Arch-
       bishop of Canterbury and the Bishop of
       Bath and Wells, because of John Stafford's
       translation from Bath and Wells to Canter-
       bury during the year]   1442–3   2 mm.

(2) *Household Account*

                                                 no. 224A
224A   Bishop Ralph of Shrewsbury   1337–8
       3 parts: Part I   4 mm.
                                                          [m.1 incomplete]
                    Part II   2 mm.
                                                          [m.1 incomplete]
                    Part III   3 mm.
       [edited by J. Armitage Robinson and A.
       Hamilton Thompson in *Collectanea* (Som-
       erset Record Society xxxix, 1924), 72–174]

(3) *Receiver's Account: general*

                                                 no. 224B
224B   Receipts from Axbridge, Banwell, Bath, Bish-
       op's Lydeard, Blackford, Buckland, Chard,
       Cheddar, Chew, Claverton, Compton,
       Congresbury, Cranmore, Draycott, Ever-
       creech, Hampton, Huish Episcopi, Kings-
       bury, Stavordale, Stoke, Stratton, Welling-
       ton, Wells, Westbury, Winscombe, Winter-
       stoke, Wookey and Yatton [all in Somerset]
       and Pucklechurch, Westerleigh and Wick
       [Glos.], followed by a rental and payments   1442–3   4 mm.
                                                    Mich.–Aug.

BATH AND WELLS ESTATES:
DEAN AND CHAPTER OF WELLS

A. COURT ROLLS
of individual properties in Somerset

BEMPSTON   no. 226

226   Hundreds [Courts and views at Burnham]   1528–9   1 m.
                                                  Sept.–April
                                                            [incomplete]

WEDMORE [BURGUS]   no. 1093

1093   Courts and views   1528–9
                                             Mich.–April   1 m.

B. ACCOUNT ROLLS
of individual properties in Somerset

CHARD PARSONAGE   no. 335

335   Bailiff   1474–5   1 m.

CURRY, EAST   no. 437

437   Reeve [? Curry Rivel also]   1415–16   2 mm. 1 att.

VI
CHICHESTER ESTATES: BISHOP

ACCOUNT ROLLS
(1) *Individual properties in Sussex*

AMBERLEY   no. 188
188   Reeve   1429-30   3 mm.

BEXHILL   nos. 247-8
247   Bedell   1429   2 pp.
248   ,,   1429-30   1 m.

FERRING   nos. 450-1
450   Reeve   1429 June-Mich. 2 pp.
451   ,,   1429-30   1 m.

HENFIELD, STREATHAM IN   no. 974
974   Reeve   1429-30   2 mm.

PRESTON   nos. 919-20
919   Bailiff   1429 June-Mich. 2 pp.
920   Reeve   1429-30   1 m.

SELSEY   nos. 951-2
951   Reeve   1429 June-Sept. 2 pp.
952   [Reeve]   [1430]   2 mm.

[Some custumals of the Bishop's manors in Sussex have been edited by W. D.
Peckham, *Sussex Record Society* xxxi, 1925]

(2) *Liberty of the Bishop*

                                                 nos. 336-7
336   Bailiff: title only [Manhood hundred also]   1428-9   1 p.
337   ,,   ,,   ,,   ,,   ,,   ,, 1429-30   1 m.

66

VII
ELY ESTATES: BISHOP

ELY ESTATES: PRIOR AND CONVENT

VIII
PRIOR AND CONVENT OF
ST BENET OF HULME, NORFOLK, ESTATES

A. COURT ROLLS
of individual properties in Norfolk

ANTINGHAM		nos. 189–90	
189	Courts	1414–16	1 m.
190	Court [headed "Antyngham Camerarii"]	1535–6	1 m.
HOUGHTON		no. 528	
528	Courts	1537–8	3 pp. [draft]
HOVETON		no. 526	
526	Courts	1416–17	1 m.
THURGARTON		no. 1074	
1074	Courts [two pedigrees of the family of atte Chambre of Martham and Skottowe, mm.8 and 9, apparently in a case about tenure in villeinage]	1413–21	17 mm.
WALSHAM		no. 1091	
1091	Courts	1440 June–July	1 m.

B. ACCOUNT ROLLS
(1) Individual properties in Norfolk

BEESTON		no. 232	
232	Rental	1374–5	1 m.
HARDLEY		no. 476	
476	Bailiff [on dorse: "Hardele et Houton"]	1356–7	4 mm.
HAUTBOIS		no. 479	
479	Serjeant	late 14th cent.	2 mm.
HOVETON, GRISHAGH IN		no. 473	
473	Rental or terrier	1392–3	1 m.
HOVETON ST JOHN		no. 527	
527	Messor	1504–5	1 m.
NEATISHEAD		nos. 755–6	
755	Rental	late 14th cent.	4 mm.
756	Messor	1504–5	1 m.

WALTON, EAST   no. 1092

1092   Rent collector and shepherd   1478–9   2 mm.

                                 no. 1437

1437   Terrier of a manor belonging to St Benet of
      Hulme   late 14th cent.   1 m.
                                      [incomplete]

(2) *Obedientiaries*

                              nos. 531–3, 1938,
                                2011, 2073

531   Cellarer [on dorse: "Hovetone, Hardelee"]   1357–8 or 1372–3 3 mm.
2073   [. . .]   [1377–8]   1 m.
532   Cellarer [on dorse: details of payments to ser-
       vants including minstrels of the Duke of
       Gloucester and of the Bishop of Norwich] 1386–7   4 mm.
533   Infirmarer   1510–11   1 m.
1938   Master of the fishery and woods   1520–1   1 m.
2011   Obedientiaries [entries relating to Anting-
       ham, Houghton and Walsham]   *c.* 1314–15   4 mm.
                                      [incomplete]
532A [Sacristan]   *temp.* Henry VI 1 m.

IX
WINCHESTER ESTATES: BISHOP

A. COURT ROLLS
of an individual property in Hampshire

FAWLEY		nos. 444–6		
444	Hundred and view	1476	1 m.	1 att.
445	,, ,, ,,	1485	1 m.	
446	Hundreds and views	1512–13	1 m.	

B. ACCOUNT ROLLS
(1) *Individual properties in Hampshire and Somerset*
Hampshire

ALRESFORD		no. 187	
187	Reeve and farmer	1490–1	3 mm.

Somerset

OTTERFORD		no. 877	
877	Reeve and farmer	1485–6	1 m.

(2) *Liberty of the Bishop*

		no. 1120	
1120	Bailiff	1537–8	1 m.

WINCHESTER ESTATES:
PRIOR AND CONVENT OF ST SWITHUN

ACCOUNT ROLLS
of individual properties in Hampshire

BARTON		no. 231	
231	Bailiff and reeve	1373	5 mm.

SILKSTEAD		nos. 949–50	
949	Farmer	1424–5	1 m.
950	,,	1444–5	1 m.

WOOTTON ST LAWRENCE		nos. 1136–7	
1136	Accounts of the grange	1401	2 mm.
1137	,, ,, ,, ,,	1426	3 mm.

X

WORCESTER ESTATES: BISHOP

COURT ROLL
of an individual property in Worcestershire

BREDON   no. 284

284   Court   1406   1 m.

WORCESTER ESTATES: PRIOR AND CONVENT

A. COURT ROLL
of an individual property in Gloucestershire

ICCOMB, CHURCH, GLOS.*   no. 540

540   Court and view [Courts at (? Almondsbury)
       and Ankerdine Hill in Doddenham]   1487–9   2 mm.
       *since 1844: previously Worcs.

B. ACCOUNT ROLLS
Obedientiaries

                                        nos. 1134–5

1134   Chamberlain   1385–6   2 mm.
1135   ,,   1437–8   3 mm.
       [A list of Chamberlains' rolls and similar
       accounts for 1521–2 have been edited by the
       Rev. J. M. Wilson, the Rev. J. H. Bloom,
       and S. G. Hamilton in *Accounts of the Priory
       of Worcester*, (Worcs. Historical Society,
       1907), pp. xi–xii and 17–20]

XI
MISCELLANEOUS ROLLS

A. COURT ROLLS

ASHWELL, HERTS.   no. 212

212   Court and view   1330 April 19   1 m.
       [Abbot and convent of St Peter, West-   Easter court
       minster]

FARMANBY, YORKS. N.R.   no. 448

448   Courts and views, and a rental   1590   2 mm.
       [Dean and Chapter of St George's Chapel,
       Windsor]

STROOD, KENT, BONCAKES MANOR AND FRANKLEYNE'S COURT IN

                                               MS. 951/1[22]
MS. 951/1[22]   Courts   1507 Dec.–   23 pp.
       [? Hospital of St Mary, Strood]   1521 Oct.   [book]

B. ACCOUNT ROLLS

BEDFORD MAJOR, PREBEND OF   no. 225
225   Rental of prebendal estates   *temp*. Robert Catesby
       [Lincoln Cathedral]   1459–87   1 m.

MILTON REGIS, KENT, RODFIELD IN   no. 943
943   Rental [with lands in Bapchild, Iwade, Mil-
       ton, Rodmersham and Sittingbourne]   1439 October 10 8 pp.

STOKE BY CLARE COLLEGE, SUFFOLK   no. 2067
2067   Provost and receiver's account   1547–8   2 mm.
       [The College was dissolved in 1548;
       Matthew Parker was dean from 1535–47]

TAVERHAM, NORFOLK, DRAYTON IN   nos. 365–78
366   Reeve   2 mm.
365   Shepherd   1432–3
367   Reeve   1433 May–Sept. 1 m.
368   Bailiff   1433–4   3 mm.
369   ,,   1435–6   6 mm.
370   Messors [Baconsthorpe also]   1441–2   3 mm.
371   Bailiff   1442–3   1 m.
372   Farmer and rent collector   1442–3   5 mm.
373   ,,   ,,   ,,   ,,   1445–6   4 mm.
374   ,,   ,,   ,,   ,,   1446–7   5 mm.
                                                1447–8   4 mm.

375	Bailiff	1450–1	5 mm. 2 pp.
376	,,	1454–5	4 mm. 1 p.
377	Bailiff and shepherd [and 3 vouchers]	1458–9	3 mm. 3 pp.
378	Bailiff	1476–7	1 m.

MS. 815

MS. 815 Rental of places in Faversham Hundred [Badlesmere, Brimstone in Oare, Ewell and Langdon in Faversham, Graveney, Oare, and Selgrave in Faversham] 1548 April 4 13 ff. [book]

no. 1448

1448 Rental: places mentioned include Great Bishopsden and Walkhurst in Benenden, Shrimpenden in Bethersden, Yardhurst and Bevenden in Great Chart [and ? Newenden in Smarden] late 15th cent. 2 pp.
[? Prior and convent of Christ Church, Canterbury]

APPENDIX A

NUMERICAL ARRANGEMENT
OF ESTATE DOCUMENTS

Christ Church Canterbury Alta Curia, Campanile Court Rolls, Obedientiaries' Accounts, Treasurers' Accounts, includes Dean and Chapter.	1–94
Liberty of the Archbishop. Accounts	95–105
Liberty of the Prior of Christ Church. Accounts	106–32
*Courts and accounts. Alphabetical order of place** chiefly Canterbury, but also other dioceses [Bath and Wells, Chichester, Ely, Winchester and St Benet of Hulme, Norfolk]	133–1158
* Except no. 452	

Grouped collections of Court Rolls

(1) Dean and Chapter of Canterbury [Kent]	1159–61
(2) Archbishop [Kent]	1162–75
(3) Bishop of Bath and Wells [Somerset]	1176–92

Grouped accounts for Archiepiscopal Manors

Ministers' accounts: various manors	1193
Ministers' accounts by bailiwicks	
Aldington	1193A–1210A
Boughton	1211
Charing	1212
Croydon	1213–21
Maidstone	1222–39
Otford	1240–59
Pagham	1260–1300
South Malling	1301–34
Wingham	1335–42
Receivers' accounts by bailiwicks	1343–77
Ministers' accounts: general	1378–1400
Receivers' accounts: general	1401–26
Imperfect *ministers' accounts*	1427–29

Documents relating to *Cartae Miscellaneae* [some retained and newly classified, the rest transferred to CMs]	1430–1558

Commonwealth Presentation Deeds
    [all transferred to that collection]
                End of Moore and Kirk's list
	1559–1773

Archiepiscopal court rolls [Kent], Ministers' and Receivers'
accounts [general], Liberty of the Archbishop [estreats]
    [Rolls transferred by the Church Commissioners from
    the Public Record Office in July 1959]
	1774–1881,
	1884–93

Archiepiscopal court rolls, Lambeth, Croydon and Waddon,
Uckfield and Ringmer, and Mayfield account
    [Rolls found in Morton's Tower among the records of
    the Vicar General in 1959]
	1895–1901

Archiepiscopal court rolls. Lambeth, Croydon and Waddon,
and Dover Priory
    [Rolls transferred by the Church Commissioners in
    January 1960]
	1902–37, 1945–72,
	1980–98, 2000–5

Miscellaneous [Documents found in the Crypt and Morton's Tower]	2006–27 [2027—fragments]

Receiver General's accounts and Deal prebend accounts
    [Documents transferred from Vicar General Tempor-
    alities]
	2028–42

Miscellaneous [Documents transferred from *Cartae Miscellaneae*]	2043–67
Archiepiscopal survey [Purchased in 1963]	2068
Miscellaneous [Documents found in 1963]	2069–73

APPENDIX B

GROUP I

Numbers of the rolls of Canterbury Archbishopric Estates [mainly Kent], transferred from the Public Record Office in July 1959, and previously in the custody of the Church Commissioners.

P.R.O. Eccles. 1/1/1	[formerly CC 90645]	now no. 1774
2	90648	1775
3	90647	1776
4	90649	1777
5	90650	1778
6	90671	1779
7	90672	1780
8	90677	1781
9	90688	1782
10	90689	1783
11	159516 2/2	1784
12	90696	1785
13	90697	1786
14	159513	1787
15	90646	1788
16	90651	1789
17	90652	1790
18	90654	1791
P.R.O. Eccles. 1/2/1	90656	1792
2	90657	1793
3	90658	1794
4	90659	1795
5	90660	1796
6	90661	1797
7	90662	1798
8	90663	1799
9	90664	1800
10	90643 1/6	1801
11	90665	1802
12	90643 6/6	1803
13	90667	1804
14	90666	1805
15	90668	1806
16	90669	1807
17	90670	1808
18	90673	1809
19	90674	1810
20	90675	1811
P.R.O. Eccles. 1/3/1	90676	1812

P.R.O. Eccles. 1/3/2	[formerly CC 90678]	now no. 1813
3	90679	1814
4	90680	1815
5	90681	1816
6	90682	1817
7	90683	1818
8	90653	1819
9	90684	1820
10	90686	1821
11	90687	1822
12	90690	1823
13	90691	1824
14	90692	1825
15	90693	1826
16	90699	1827
P.R.O. Eccles. 1/4/1	90694	1828
2	90695	1829
3	90685	1830
4	90698	1831
5	90700	1832
6	90701	1833
7	90702	1834
8	90705	1835
9	90706	1836
10	90708	1837
11	90709	1838
12	90710	1839
13	90711	1840
14	90713	1841
P.R.O. Eccles. 1/5/1	90714	1842
2	90715	1843
3	90716	1844
4	90717	1845
5	90718	1846
6	90719	1847
7	90720	1848
8	90722	1849
9	90723	1850
10	90724	1851
P.R.O. Eccles. 1/6/1	90726	1852
2	90727	1853
3	90728	1854
4	90729	1855
5	90730	1856
6	90731	1857
7	90733	1858
8	90734	1859
9	90735	1860
10	90736	1861
P.R.O. Eccles. 1/7/1	90737	1862
2	90738	1863

P.R.O. Eccles. 1/7/3	[formerly CC 90739]	now no. 1864
4	90740	1865
5	90741	1866
6	90742	1867
7	90743	1868
8	90744	1869
9	90745	1870
10	90746	1871
P.R.O. Eccles. 1/8/1	90747	1872
2	90748	1873
3	90749	1874
4	90750	1875
5	90751	1876
6	90752	1877
7	90753	1878
8	90754	1879
9	90755	1880
10	90756	1881
P.R.O. Eccles. 2/123	90643 5/6	1884
,,	90655	1885
,,	90703	1886
,,	90704	1887
,,	90707	1888
,,	90712	1889
,,	90721	1890
,,	90725	1891
,,	90730a	1892
,,	90732	1893

GROUP II

Numbers of the rolls and books of Canterbury Archbishopric Estates [Lambeth, Croydon and Waddon, and Dover Priory], transferred from the Church Commissioners in January 1960.

CC		now no.	CC	now no.
87689		2003	171189	1910
87690		2004	171191	1911
87691		2005	171192	1912
98890a	1/3	2000	171193	1913
98890a	2/3	2001	171194	1914
98890a	3/3	2002	171195	1915
171184	1/4	1905	171196	1916
171184	2/4	1906	171197	1917
171184	3/4	1902	171198	1918
171184	4/4	1904	171199	1919
171184	5/4	1903	171200	1920
171185		1906a	171201	1921
171186		1907	171202	1922
171187		1908	171203	1923
171188		1909	171204	1924

CC 171205	now no. 1925	CC 171252	now no. 1963
171206	1926	171253	1964
171207	1927	171254	1965
171208	1928	171257	1966
171209	1929	171257	1967
171210	1930	171257	1968
171211	1931	171257	1969
171212	1932	171258	1970
171214	1933	171258	1971
171214	1934	171258	1972
171214	1935	414071	1980a
171214	1936	414072	1980
171214	1937	414073	1981
171235	1945	414074	1982
171236	1946	414075	1983
171237	1947	414076	1984
171238	1948	414077	1985
171239	1949	414078	1986
171240	1950	414079	1987
171241	1951	414080	1988
171242	1952	414081	1989
171243	1953	414082	1990
171244	1954	414083	1991
171244a	1955	414084	1992
171245	1956	414085	1993
171246	1957	414090	1994
171247	1958	414091	1995
171248	1959	414092	1996
171249	1960	414093	1997
171250	1961	415771	1998
171251	1962		

GROUP III

Numbers of the rolls etc. formerly in the collection of Cartae Miscellaneae.

CM VI/86 f	now no. 2049	CM XIII/22	now no. 2054
X/130	2050	XIII/30	2066
X/150	2051	XIII/31	2047
XI/89	2063	XIII/32	2046
XI/90	2053	XIII/33	2064
XI/91	2052	XIII/34	2045
XII/10	2060	XIII/35	2048
XIII/5	452	XIII/36	2044
XIII/8	2065	XIII/39	2056
XIII/10	2062	XIII/41	2057
XIII/11	2043	XIII/45	2059
XIII/12	2058	XIII/46	2061
XIII/14 (see X/150)	2051	XIII/64	2067
XIII/18	2055		

Unused Numbers

256

1430–4	Documents now transferred to the collection of *Cartae Miscellaneae* listed in Moore and Kirk's Calendar.
1435	now MS. 1681: referred to in Moore and Kirk's Calendar.
1436	
1438–41	
1443–7	Documents now transferred to the collection of *Cartae Miscellaneae*
1450–7	listed in Moore and Kirk's Calendar.
1459–63	
1465–73	
1465–1558	
1559–1773	Documents now transferred to the collection of Commonwealth Presentation Deeds: listed in Lambeth Palace Library, Catalogue of Commonwealth Ecclesiastical Records.
1882	now CM XIII/77: formerly CC 90643 2/6.
1883	now CM XIII/78: formerly CC 90643 3/6.
1894	
1942–4	Documents now transferred to the collection of the Records of the Church Commissioners: listed in Lambeth Palace Library, Catalogue of the Records of the Church Commissioners for England for the Archiepiscopate of Canterbury.
1974–9	

Missing Rolls

103   347A

Manuscripts composed of, or containing, Estate Documents

MSS. 789–841 form part of the Tenison collection; MS. 942 is a Gibson manuscript, and MSS. 951–1094 are from the miscellaneous collection. They have been described, sometimes very inaccurately, in Henry Todd's *Catalogue of the Archiepiscopal Manuscripts*, London, 1812. They retain their manuscript numbers, but have been re-described in their appropriate places above.

MS. 789	MS. 815	MS. 952[5]
790	833	[38]
791	841[22]	[53]
792	942[10]	[54]
793	951/1[22]	[93]
794	[30]	1025[1]
795	[31]	[6]
796	[32]	[7]
797	[33]	[8]
798	[34]	1094[2]
814	952[3]	[12]

INDEX OF PLACES

G

INDEX

Buckland, [West], Somerset **60, 61, 62,** 63, 64
Buckland [in Dover]; see *Dover*
Burmarsh, Willop in 30, **31**; see also *Aldington bailiwick*
Burnham, Somerset 65
Burstow, Surrey 25, **26,** 31, **32**; see also *Croydon bailiwick*

Caldicote [in Canterbury]; see *Canterbury*
Calehill 2, 3, **4**
Canons Court [*al*. Blackwose]; see *Saltwood*
Canterbury 56; Archbishop's Palace in 2, 18, 36; see also *Wingham bailiwick*; Caldicote [*al*. St Martin's] in 30, 45, 47, 55; Eastbridge Hospital in 18
Canterbury, St Augustine's Abbey 59
Canterbury, St Gregory's bailiwick **39, 41**
Canterbury, St Sepulchre's Priory **39**
Canterbury, Westgate 2, **13,** 18, 30, **36, 39, 41**; Shulford Mead in **41, 43**; see also *Wingham bailiwick*
Capel le Ferne **43**; Satmar in **14,** 37, **39, 42**
Chalk, Filborough in 45
Challock **39, 41,** 52
Chard, Somerset 60, 61, **62,** 64, 65
Charing **2, 4,** 18, 30, 32, **33**; Newland in 2; see also *Maidstone bailiwick*
Charing bailiwick 32
Charlton [in Dover]; see *Dover*
Chart, Great 45, 47, **55**; Bevenden in 73; Yardhurst in 73
Chart, Little 52
Chartham **55, 56**
Cheam, Surrey 25, 30, **32**; see also *Croydon bailiwick*
Cheddar, Somerset 61, **62,** 63, 64
Cheriton, Enbrook in **37, 39**
Chevening **34**; see also *Otford bailiwick*
Chew [Magna], Somerset 60, **62,** 64
Cheyne Court [in Ivychurch]; see *Ivychurch*
Cheyne Marsh [in Ivychurch]; see *Ivychurch*
Chichester, the Pallant, Sussex **10, 11**
Chislet **14, 37, 39, 41**; see also *Wingham, Chislet and West Langdon bailiwick*
Church Iccomb; see *Iccomb, Church*
Claverton; see *Hampton and Claverton*
Cliffe, West, near Dover 47
Cliffe, West, near Rochester; see *Cliffe at Hoo*
Cliffe at Hoo [*al*. West Cliffe near Rochester] 1, **2,** 3, **6, 45,** 52; Bishop's Marsh in 19, 21, **34**; Little Harsyng Marsh in 21; see also *Iwade, Hersing Marsh in* and *Otford bailiwick*

Codsheath 2, **5,** 6
Coldred **37, 39, 41**
Combe [in Newington next Hythe]; see *Newington next Hythe*
Compton Bishop, Somerset 60, 61, **62,** 63, 64
Congresbury and Yatton, Somerset **60, 62,** 64
Copton [in Preston]; see *Preston next Faversham*
Cornard, Great, Suffolk **39**
Court Ash [in Upper Deal]; see *Deal, Upper*
Court-at-Street [in Lympne]; see *Lympne*
Cranbrook 19, **31**; see also *Aldington bailiwick*
Cranmore, Somerset **61, 62, 64**
Craphill [in Wye]; see *Wye*
Crayford **2,** 3, 6; Earde in 1, **5**
Croydon, Surrey 8, 25, 30, 31, **32, 40,** 42; Purley in **39, 42**; Selhurst in **39, 40, 42**; Waddon in 25, **32, 40, 42**; see also *Croydon bailiwick* and *Croydon and Waddon*
Croydon bailiwick 30, **32, 37**
Croydon and Waddon, Surrey 7, **16**
Curlswood [in Nonington]; see *Nonington*
Curry, East, Somerset 65
Curry Rivel, Somerset 65

Dane Court [in St Peters]; see *St Peters*
Deal 30, **36**; see also *Wingham bailiwick*
Deal, Upper 3; Court Ash in 3
Deal Prebend **13,** 19, **40, 41**
Doccombe, Devon 46, 55
Doddenham, Worcestershire, Ankerdine Hill in 71
Doddington, Isle of Ely, Cambridgeshire 67
Doddington **44**; Oakenpole in 33; see also *Maidstone bailiwick*
Dogmersfield, Hampshire 63
Dover 37, **39, 41**; Buckland in 43; Buckland, Dudmanscombe in 3; Charlton in 44
Dover Priory 3
Down Barton [in St Nicholas at Wade]; see *St Nicholas at Wade*
Downham, Isle of Ely, Cambridgeshire 67
Draycott [? in Rodney Stoke]; see *Stoke*
Drayton [in Taverham]; see *Taverham*
Dudmanscombe [in Buckland]; see *Dover, Buckland*
Dunkirk, North Bishopsden Wood in **41**; North and South Bishopsden Woods in 36; see also *Wingham bailiwick*

Earde [in Crayford]; see *Crayford*
East Curry; see *Curry, East*

82